The Wise Owl Guide to…

DANTES Subject Standardized Test (DSST)

Human Resource Management

ISBN-10: 1449590489
ISBN-13: 9781449590482
Library of Congress Control Number: 2010901905

TABLE OF CONTENTS

INTRODUCTION

Are you going to learn everything about human resource management in this study guide? Absolutely not! But... are you going to learn enough to pass the DSST test? Yes! This guide's focus is the test. The DSST (Dantes Subject Standardized Test) series tests cover what is most commonly taught in a college course. That leaves out a lot of content that might be taught in a formal class. Prepare for this test with this study guide and you will be well on your way to a degree in significantly less time than hitting the books in night school (this is not to say it is any easier to get a degree this way, just more flexible)! This book is written in a format that's easy-to-read, understand, and remember. Human resource management is a fascinating topic, and no matter if you have a test to pass or not this information will make you feel like a more educated person for knowing it. Even if you *think* you know everything there is to know about human resource management, this book will teach you a thing or two!

USING THIS GUIDE

First, this study guide is not a textbook. It is a study guide that will help you identify the most important (and most heavily tested) topics in the human resource management course. If you feel the need, you can purchase a textbook (it doesn't have to be the latest edition) in order to gain an in-depth look into human resource management. Then, you can follow along with this study guide to help you pull out the exact information you need in order to pass the test. What you do depends on your goal. Are you in it simply for the credits, or do you also enjoy the process of learning? There is no right or wrong answer to this question.

ABOUT THE TEST

The American Council of Education (ACE) recommends three lower level baccalaureate credits in business. However, before using this or any study guide ensure your school accepts this test for credit. This test and book cover the following topics:

- Overview of the human resource management field
- Human resource planning
- Staffing
- Training and development
- Performance appraisals
- Compensation issues
- Safety and health
- Employee rights and discipline
- Employment law
- Labor relations
- International human resource management
- Current issues and trends

This test book includes a 100-question practice test to ensure you have a solid handle on the course information.

PART I OVERVIEW OF THE HUMAN RESOURCE
MANAGEMENT FIELD

Part I accounts for approximately four percent of the test. This
section will cover:

- Historical development
- Human resource functions
- Human resource manager
- Motivation, communication, and leadership
- Ethics of human resource decision making

The goal of studying human resource management is to have a
competitive advantage over other organizations through people. By
focusing on **core competencies** (an integrated knowledge within
an organization that sets it out from the competition) an
organization can succeed. A strong core competency is:
- Valuable
- Rare
- Hard to copy
- Organized

HISTORICAL DEVELOPMENT

The Industrial Revolution triggered a shift from working in the
home to working in factories, steel mills, and railroads. Out of this
new work environment grew a need for managing people within an
organization.
- The period that saw the growth of factories from the 1900s
  through the 1940s led to the development of personnel
  programs, the passing of key legislation and the
  establishment of a guiding set of human resource
  management social science principles.
- Industrial psychology was born between 1910 and 1930
  when companies began to devote entire departments to the
  maintenance of worker welfare.
- The human resource management field saw several new
  developments during the 1920s and 1930s:
  - On-the-job training programs were started.
  - Studies were conducted.
    - **Informal factors** include the social
      environment of the workplace and informal
      work groups.

- In 1927, research, conducted by Elton Mayo and his associates, began at the Hawthorne Plant of the Western Electric Company in an attempt to investigate the role that physical factors play in productivity.

HUMAN RESOURCE FUNCTIONS

The functions of human resource management generally include three phases:
- Pre-hire
  - Planning
  - Developing career paths within the organization.
  - Jobs within an organization may or may not be part of a career path.

- Hire
  - Staffing
    - Includes recruitment and selection processes, requires that the human resource manager determine the type and number of individuals needed to get the job done.
    - Designs individual jobs and accurately describes duties by way of a job description.
      - **Job description** includes tasks, responsibilities and minimum required experience.
    - Recruitment of individuals can occur within or outside of the organization.
    - The process of screening, interviewing and hiring individuals is known as **selection**.
    - The best tool for determining the hire that is the right fit for the company is the job interview, which can come in the form of a structured interview, an unstructured interview or a stress interview.
    - Human resource managers can help an organization sustain a competitive advantage through their people by recruiting and maintaining people that are:
      - Valuable (efficient and effective)

- Rare (have an uncommon set of skills, knowledge, and abilities)
- Organized (talents must be able to be used for the right job and quickly to maintain a nimble organization)
- Post-hire
  - Training and development
    - Designed to aid managers in helping their employees to develop key skills for better performance.
    - Training methods should be tailored to meet individual needs based on the present stage of the worker's career.
    - Training can be performed "on-the-job" or "off-the-job," depending on the specific developmental needs of the company and individuals within the organization.
  - Performance appraisals
    - Management's best tool for measuring individual accomplishment is the performance appraisal.
  - Compensation issues
    - **Compensation** can come in the form of cash compensation or non-cash compensation.
      - **Cash compensation** includes hourly wages, salaries and bonuses.
      - **Non-cash compensation** includes other employee benefits, such as health insurance, pension contributions, tuition reimbursement, and legal assistance programs.
    - A company's ability to pay and its level of productivity, supply and demand, labor unions and governmental regulations are all factors that impact compensation and must be taken into consideration by human resource managers dealing with compensatory issues of an organization.
  - Researching and auditing

- Research can be conducted in the form of historical studies, surveys and controlled experiments.
- Audits may be conducted on individual departments or they can be companywide.
  - Separations
    - **Separations** refer to the different conditions under which someone leaves a company.
    - Separations can be voluntary or involuntary, and may occur at any level of an organization.
      - Resignations, retirement, reductions in force (RIF) or lay-offs, and discharges are the different ways that people may leave an organization.

HUMAN RESOURCE MANAGER

Human resource managers are responsible for:
- Advice and counsel
  - Advise managers and supervisors of internal employment issues and helping managers reach the goals of organizations through people.
- Service
  - Provide services for the organization such as:
    - Recruitment
    - Selection
    - Testing
    - Planning training
    - Fielding employee concerns
- Policy
  - Human resource managers propose new policies and (once approved) implement them for the organization.
- Employee advocacy
  - They listen to employee concerns and represent employees when talking to management.

Successful HR managers have several common traits:
- Business knowledge
  - Understand the business their organization is in.
  - Understand the economic and financial capabilities of the organization.
- Human relation knowledge

- o Understand organizational science on staffing, development, appraisal, rewards, teams, and communications.
- Change ability
  - o Have the ability to implement change and apply problem-solving skills.
- Personal credibility
  - o Human resource managers exhibit personal credibility by developing personal relationships, standing up for their beliefs, and exhibiting fairness.

MOTIVATION, COMMUNICATION, AND LEADERSHIP

The ability to motivate, communicate, and lead are important skills/traits for the successful human resource manager.

MOTIVATION

Motivating people to achieve organizational goals influences productivity and ultimately the success of a manager. Motivation comes from two places:

- **Intrinsic rewards**
  - o The positive feeling someone has while performing the action.
- **Extrinsic rewards**
  - o A reward given to someone after the completion of an action.

MOTIVATION APPROACHES

There are four main approaches (schools of thought) on motivation:

- **Traditional**
  - Economic rewards are used to motivate employees to perform.
- **Human relations**
  - Treatment of employees (social, work groups, and noneconomic rewards) motivates employees to perform.
- **Human resources**
  - People want to do a good job because work is natural and healthy.
  - Treat the person as a whole with a mix of the noneconomic and economic rewards.
- **Contemporary**
  - Content theories
    - Abraham Maslow **Hierarchy of Needs theory**
      - People are motivated by needs in the following order: physiological, safety, belonging, esteem, and self-actualization.
    - **ERG theory**
      - Modification of Maslow's Hierarchy of Needs.
      - People are motivated by three categories:
        - Existence
        - Relatedness
        - Growth
    - **Theory X and Theory Y theory**
      - Coined by Douglas McGregor.
      - Theory X assumes that people are lazy and must be coerced.
      - Theory Y assumes that people enjoy work and can self-direct.
    - **Two-Factor theory**
      - Coined by Frederick Herzberg.
      - **Hygiene factors** (working conditions, pay, company policies, and interpersonal relationships). They eliminate job dissatisfaction, but do not motivate the employee.

13

- **Motivators** (need for achievement, recognition, responsibility, and growth). Factors that both eliminate job dissatisfaction and stimulate motivation.
  - **Acquired Needs theory (Three Needs theory)**
    - Coined by David McClelland.
    - **Need for achievement** (want to accomplish something hard to obtain)
    - **Need for affiliation** (want to foster close relationships)
    - **Need for power** (want to control others)
- Process theory
  - **Equity theory**
    - Focuses on if individuals think they are being treated fairly.
    - People will strive for equality and will either increase or decrease their productivity (**change inputs**), try to resolve the inequality outright (**change outcomes**), or if they can't do either, they may **distort their perceptions** of the inequality, or leave their job.
  - **Expectancy theory**
    - Focuses motivation on receiving rewards.
    - How the individual thinks their effort will affect the outcomes supplies motivation.
- Reinforcement theory
  - Reinforcement theories focus on behavior and consequences.
    - **Positive reinforcement** is a reward for desired behavior.
    - **Negative reinforcement** is the removal of something unpleasant with a desired behavior.

- **Punishment** is giving something unpleasant for an undesired behavior.
- **Extinction** is the withdrawal of a reward.
- Reinforcement schedules are different and have varying effectiveness.
    - **Continuous reinforcement** is when every desired behavior is reinforced. It is effective when the behavior is new.
    - **Partial reinforcement** is when some of the desired behavior is reinforced. There are four types of schedules:
        - **Fixed-interval** – gives reward at specific time intervals (pay checks). Results in average and irregular performance.
        - **Fixed-ratio**- gives reward after specific number of desired behaviors. Results in high and stable performance.
        - **Variable**-interval – random times not picked by employee. Results in moderately high and stable performance.
        - **Variable**-ratio – random number of behaviors. Results in very high performance.

COMMUNICATION

It is important for a human resource manager to be able to express ideas effectively through oral and written communication. Communication serves several purposes:
- Unites employees within all levels of management.
- Ensures everyone realizes a shared goal.
- Mechanism for reporting progress.

LEADERSHIP

Although all managers must lead in some way, not all managers are leaders. **Leadership** is the ability to influence people to achieve goals for the organization. A significant difference between a manager and a leader is the source of their power. Management power is by the position in the organization, while leadership power comes from personal sources. There are three types of power that come from the position in an organization:
- **Legitimate**
  - Built into the structure of the organization and is dependent upon one's position within the company.
- **Reward**
  - Built into the organizational structure, and is the control that management has over rewarding subordinates.
- **Coercive**
  - Built into the organizational structure, and is the control that management has over punishing subordinates.

There are two types of power that come from personal sources:
- **Expert**
  - Based on individual expertise.
  - The amount expert power one possesses is based on skill, knowledge, ability and experience.
- **Referent**
  - The degree in which the person is admired and people want to emulate them.

The three basic types of leadership are:
- **Authoritarian**
    - o Characterized by dictatorship that dismisses input from team members.
    - o Decides the terms of tasks and who will perform the work to be done.
- **Democratic**
    - o Characterized by an open-line of communication between workers and management.
    - o Values team-input, and facilitates group cooperation without being overly active within the group.
- **Laissez-faire**
    - o Hands off approach over all decision-making without any further involvement unless asked to participate.

There are several types of leaders, and not any one leader would be effective in all management situations. The types of leaders include:
- **Transactional leader**
    - o Clarifies the roles, initiates structure, provides rewards, and is considerate of employees.
    - o They are fair, hardworking and tolerant leaders.
    - o Emphasis on job-oriented (not personal) needs.
- **Charismatic leader**
    - o Characterized by the ability to motivate employees to go beyond expectations.
    - o Emphasizes inspiration, vision, and leading by example.
    - o Charismatic leaders are less predictable than transactional leaders and embrace new ideas.
    - o Charismatic leaders are visionaries and they try to get others to see a better future and their participation in it.

- **Transformational leader**
  - o Characterized by their ability to bring innovation by recognizing needs of the employees.
  - o Looks at old problems in new ways and seeks creative solutions.
- **Servant leader**
  - o Characterized by their prioritization on fulfilling employees' needs and goals balanced with the organizational mission.
  - o Subordinate, customer, and community needs are placed above the leader's own needs.

LEADERSHIP IN THEORY

There is no one right approach to leadership; however most agree that managers can learn to become leaders, although where emphasis is placed differs from one approach to the next.

- Trait theories
  - o Emphasize characteristics that separate leaders from non-leaders.
- Behavioral theories
  - o Emphasize task-oriented and relationship oriented behavioral differences between effective and ineffective leaders, stressing that leadership can be learned.
- Situational theories
  - o Stress situational variables, rather than characteristics of the individual manager.
  - o Links leadership with the leader's behavior and the readiness of the staff.
  - o **Fiedler's Contingency Model**
    - ▪ Matches the leader style with the situation that is conducive to it.
  - o **Path-Goal Theory**
    - ▪ Contingency approach that specifies that the leader is responsible to increase motivation by clarifying the path and increasing the rewards.
    - ▪ Four leadership behaviors:
      - • **Directive**

- o Clear expectations, schedules, and specific guidance
- **Supportive**
  - o Friendliness and concern
- **Participative**
  - o Consults group and uses suggestions when making a decision
- **Achievement oriented**
  - o Sets challenging goals

ETHICS OF HUMAN RESOURCE DECISION MAKING

Although the main goal of human resource management is to advance the organization's advantage in a competitive business world, HR is also responsible for acting ethically in decision-making practices. There are three roles the human resource professional plays in the arena of workplace ethics:

- Monitor
  - o Watches actions of the personnel to ensure ethical and fair treatment of workers.
- Investigator
  - o Investigates complaints of unfair treatment.
- Spokesperson.
  - o Represents the organization when approached by media or regulatory agencies.

Business ethics is a code of moral principles and values that govern organizational behavior. Organizations face frequent **ethical dilemmas** (all choices are deemed undesirable for potential harmful consequences). Nearly all-human resource decisions have an ethical component.

TYPES OF ETHICAL DECISIONS

Ethical decisions typically have two sides to the equation the individual versus the organization. There are five main approaches to ethical decisions, they are:

- **Utilitarian**
  - o Coined by John Stuart Mill.
  - o Behavior that causes the greatest good for the most is ethical.
- **Individualism**

- - Morality is based on the long-term interests of an individual.
  - Usually supports honesty and integrity.
    - For example, while cheating may initially give someone a leg-up, in the long run, it will only do harm.
- **Integrative social contracts theory**
  - Ethical decisions are based on existing norms.
- **Moral –rights**
  - Humans have fundamental rights that should be considered:
    - Consent
    - Privacy
    - Conscience (should not have to carry out any order that mollifies their conscience)
    - Free speech
    - Due process
    - Life and safety
- **Justice**
  - Decisions should be completely impartial.

ABILITY TO MAKE ETHICAL DECISIONS

There are several factors that play a role in the ability for individuals to act ethically including moral development, individual characteristics, structural variables, organizational culture, and the intensity of the issue.

MORAL DEVELOPMENT

The stage of moral development has a direct impact on the ability to make moral decisions:
- **Preconventional**
  - Person is only concerned with external rewards and punishments.
  - Characteristic of managers that use authoritative and coercive styles.
- **Conventional**
  - Learn to conform from the expectations of those around them.
  - Meeting social and interpersonal obligations is of the greatest importance.
  - Work collaboration is preferred.

- **Postconventional/principled**
  - o Guided by an internal set of values and beliefs.
  - o Characteristic of managers that encourage the staff to think for themselves and engage in moral reasoning.

Most people are at the second/conventional level of development.

INDIVIDUAL CHARACTERISTICS

Before people join an organization they typically have their own set of values. **Values** are the basic individual beliefs about what is right and wrong. Usually values are developed throughout childhood from family, peers, and teachers. Two specific personality traits that influence a person's value system are:

- **Ego strength**
  - o The strength of a person's convictions.
  - o People who have high ego strength typically will follow what they believe is ethical in lieu of following unethical impulses.
- **Locus of control**
  - o Degree to which an individual believes they have control of their fate.
  - o An **external locus** believes that things happen due to luck or chance.
    - External locus people believe in limited accountability for their actions.
  - o An **internal locus** believes that things happen because they made it happen.
    - Internal locus individuals are typically more ethical than those that are external.

STRUCTURAL VARIABLES

Organizational structure can impact ethics within the organization.

- Strong guidance (formal rules and regulations) can increase probability of ethical decisions.
- Performance appraisals
  - o Focusing on the means as well as the outcome can increase the likelihood of ethical behavior.
  - o Conversely, focusing solely on the outcomes can increase unethical behavior.
- Supervisors

21

- Managerial behavior is the single most relevant indicator of ethical behavior of the staff.

ORGANIZATIONAL CULTURE

Organizations will likely get ethical behaviors if they have high risk, control, and conflict tolerance.

ISSUE INTENSITY

The intensity of the issue will influence an organization's member's ethical response. For example, an employee who believes embezzlement is bad may pilfer office supplies. Both situations are ethically stealing, however one is obviously more intense than the other. There are six main factors that influence issue intensity:

- Greatness of harm
  - Amount of people that it would harm.
- Consensus of wrong
  - The amount of people that view the act as wrong.
- Probability of harm
  - Likelihood that the action will cause harm.
- Consequence immediacy
  - How quickly the consequences for an unethical act will be felt.
- Victim proximity
  - The person's feelings for the victim.
- Effect concentration
  - The concentration of the act on the victim.

Part II Human Resource Planning

Part II accounts for approximately six percent of the test. This section will cover:

- Strategic human resource issues
- Job analysis and job design

While planning is involved at all levels of management, each manager's job is to plan for their specific unit. Human resource managers focus on people and getting the right person in the right job.

Strategic human resource issues

Strategic planning is reserved for the highest levels of management. The plans are long-term (longer than five years), and take into account the organization's mission. Since human capital is the single most important resource an organization has, the human resources has a special function in the strategic planning process, including:

- Career path
- Job design
- Recruitment
- Performance appraisals
- Design and implementation of rewards
- **Succession planning** (identification of future candidates for future anticipated vacancies)

Job analysis and job design

Human resource management's role in **job analysis** involves determining the type and number of individuals needed to get the job done. Designing individual jobs and accurately describing job duties via a detailed job description that spells out tasks, responsibilities and minimum required experience, as well as the way the job should be completed are all components of human resource job design. Today, job designers tend to focus on job enrichment and teamwork when developing new positions within their organizations, instead of relying on the traditional model, which based job design on the principles of division of labor and specialization that aimed to narrow job content as much as possible.

There are four main approaches to job analysis:
- **Functional job analysis (FJA)**
  - Quantitative approach to job analysis that assumes all parts of the job relate to data, people, and things.
  - Compiled inventory of the functions of a job based on three categories.
- **Position analysis questionnaire (PAQ)**
  - 194-point questionnaire with five-point scale to determine the degree in which tasks are performed.
- **Critical incident method**
  - Job identified by the tasks that make it a success.
- **Computerized job analysis**
  - Various software programs that write job description and specifications based on the job analysis.

Job design is investigated to keep employees motivated to achieve the management goals. Job design includes job simplification, job rotation, job enlargement, and job enrichment.
- **Job simplification**
  - Improvement of efficiency by simplifying it (standardized, repetitive, and simple are the goals of job simplification).
  - Typically fails because people do not want boring jobs.
  - People rebel by calling in sick, joining unions, and sabotaging their job.
- **Job rotation**
  - Moves an employee into different jobs for variety.
  - Once repetitive work is mastered boredom sets in.
- **Job enlargement**
  - Makes a job more complex.
  - Improves the level of boredom in an oversimplified job.
- **Job enrichment**
  - Uses motivators (responsibility, recognition, growth) to increase satisfaction.

Richard Hackman and Greg Oldham researched job design and motivation and came up with the **Characteristics Model**. The Characteristics model focuses on three parts:
- Core job dimensions

- Skill variety
  - Routine jobs are low in variety.
- Task identity
  - The degree which employee performs a job from beginning to end.
- Task significance
  - The degree which employees perceive the importance of a job.
- Autonomy
  - The degree which employees have freedom over their job.
- Feedback
  - Amount of information employee receives for their job.
- Critical psychological states
  - Meaningfulness
    - Intrinsic rewards is experienced.
  - Responsibility for outcome
    - Related to the core job dimension of autonomy.
  - Knowledge of results
    - Related to the core job dimension of feedback.
- Employee growth need
  - People have different needs for growth and development.

PART III STAFFING

Part III accounts for approximately fifteen percent of the test. This section will cover:

- Recruiting
- Selection
- Promotions and transfers
- Reduction-in-force
- Voluntary turnover

RECRUITING

Recruitment is a task that every manager performs. Before a manager can successfully recruit a candidate she or he needs to know the job specifications for the position. **Job specifications** are the knowledge, skills, and abilities needed to successfully fill the position. The purpose of advertising the specifications for the position is to attract the right candidate for the right job.

- **Human resource planning** is the matching of people with future vacancies.
- Promoting existing staff into higher positions.
- **Recruiting** is defining the characteristics that the organization feels would be a good fit for the vacancies. To recruit the right people an organization must:
  - o Conduct **job analysis** to understand the duties of a job.
  - o Provide a summary of the position in a **job description**.
  - o Give a **job specification** that outlines the knowledge, skills, and abilities required for the job.

Employees are recruited to positions from within or outside an organization. When recruiting from outside the organization several techniques are commonly employed, such as:

- Placing an advertisement
- Headhunters (helps job seekers find the right job)
- Utilizing employment agencies
- Current employee referrals
  - o Pay the employee for a successful placement.
  - o Save some of the referral bonus for after six months (to ensure the hire is a good fit).
  - o Tailor the program to strongly desired skills.

- Recruiting through other organizations (e.g. colleges and professional organizations)

SELECTION

Managers usually prefer to hire or promote from within by way of an internal job posting or through searching and evaluating existing employee files, referred to as **internal selection**. During the process of selection, potential employees are screened and interviewed in order to make a hiring decision. The human resource manager has a great responsibility during selection. The HR manager must fully comply with the all federal and state statutes. The selection process includes a **job description**, which is a declaration of the tasks and responsibilities of the job. There are several steps to facilitate the selection process, often dependent on the nature of the position to be filled.

- Screening
  - Also known as initial reception or first-impression.
- Testing
  - Sometimes required before the potential hire is invited to advance to the interviewing stage of the process.
- Background check
  - Depending on company HRM practices and the requirements of the job, a reference and/or background check may be completed, as well as a medical examination performed before a decision to hire is made.
  - Background and reference checks may include:
    - Personal references
    - Previous employers
    - Credit check
    - Criminal convictions check
    - Driving records
- Interview
  - The interview is the single most important tool in making a decision to select a candidate.

- o There are three main types of interviews:
  - **Structured**
    - Management uses a set group of questions so they can compare the answers across all candidates.
    - The four types of questions asked are:
      - o Job knowledge
      - o Job simulation
      - o Situational
      - o Work willingness
  - **Unstructured**
    - May have no format at all, or be open-ended questions.
    - Unstructured interviews make it difficult to compare candidates.
  - **Stress**
    - Places the applicant in a simulated high stress setting to interview the candidate.
- Selecting the candidate
  - o The most common method of selecting a candidate is via the written offer letter.

Upon selection of a candidate HR must validate the selected candidate is a United States citizen (or legally able to work in the United States). HR has the following responsibilities:

- Instruct employees to fill out a Form I-9.
- Check documentation establishing identity.
- Complete the employer portion of the I-9.
- Retain I-9 for three years.
- Present I-9 to the federal government upon request.

UNIFORM GUIDELINES ON EMPLOYEE SELECTION PROCEDURES

HR managers are sometimes uncertain about the appropriateness of certain selection procedures. To help guide them in an ethical decision of selection they sometimes refer to the Uniform Guidelines on Employee Selection Procedures. **Uniform Guidelines on Employee Selection Procedures** is a procedural document designed by the federal government to assist in hiring, retention, promotion, transfer, demotion, dismissal, and referrals.

Some of the highlights of the document are the following definitions:

- **Adverse impact**
  - o Rejection of a higher percentage of protected classes for employment.
  - o Unintentional discrimination.
- **Four-fifths rule**
  - o Selection of a minority is less than 80 percent of the time.
  - o Rule of thumb in determining adverse impact during proceedings.
- **Restricted policy**
  - o Evidence suggesting selection precludes members from protected classes.
  - o **Disparate treatment**
    - ▪ Purposeful discrimination.
  - o People that think they have been the subject of discrimination can file a suit if they pass the **McDonnell Douglas Test**:
    - ▪ Member of a protected class
    - ▪ Applied for a job they were qualified for
    - ▪ Rejected (despite qualifications)
    - ▪ After rejection the employer sought applicants with same qualifications.

PROMOTIONS AND TRANSFERS

Promotions and transfers are recruitment from within the organization. Organizations will communicate information about job openings (**job posting and bidding**) in the organization. Some advantages of recruitment from within are:

- Reward and motivate employees
- Improving morale within the organization
- While transfers are not as motivating they too can be a reward to:
  - o Avoid a lay off
  - o Broaden job experience
  - o Eliminate the training and orientation costs of a new employee
  - o The HR manager will have a likely indicator of the person's success within the organization based on past experiences.

Some limitations of recruitment from within are:

- Sometimes no one in the organization has the skill set needed (especially for smaller organizations).
- Skill sets from another organization are required.
  - Sometimes high-tech companies will hire former employees of another company in an attempt to access trade secrets.

REDUCTION-IN-FORCE

Reduction-in-force (RIF) can be voluntary or involuntary.
- Voluntary reductions in force often include some type of severance pay and extension of benefits for a predetermined period of time.
  - In some instances, outplacement services are extended to employees to encourage them to leave the organization.
  - Taking an "early retirement" package from a company is an example of a voluntary separation.
  - Voluntary separation by way of reduction in force is voluntary in the sense that the employee volunteers to leave the organization due to incentives offered.
- Involuntary reductions on the other hand are composed of lay-offs, either across-the-board or through company reorganization that result in fewer available positions.
  - Determining the order for laying-off employees differs from one company to the next depending on organizational Human Resource Management policies.

AVOIDING LEGAL ISSUES DURING LAYOFFS

Massive layoffs can lead to legal issues. There are several ways that employers can reduce the likelihood of lawsuit.
- Document business reasons for lay off.
- Focus on positions to be eliminated not people.
- Get outside consultation on layoffs of personnel.
- Ensure layoffs are not discriminatory in nature.
- Offer severance packages to encourage voluntary separations.

Voluntary turnover from an organization come in the form of:

- Resignations
    - Intent to resign from a company is typically expressed in a written communication to the employee's manager.
    - Generally, the written notice of resignation will include:
        - Statement of the employee's intent to leave.
        - Specific final date of employment (usually two or more weeks after notification).
    - While resignations are always voluntary, there are two types:
        - **Unencouraged resignation**
            - When an employee chooses to resign without provocation from the employer.
        - **Encouraged resignation**
            - When an employer suggests resignation to an employee.
- Retirement
    - Retirement separations are typically planned well in advance, and are well-received, celebratory occasions.
    - Organizations can typically prepare for retirement turnover.

PART IV TRAINING AND DEVELOPMENT

Part IV accounts for approximately eleven percent of the test. This section will cover:

- Orientation
- Career planning
- Principles of learning
- Training programs and methods
- Development programs

ORIENTATION

Orientation is an on-the-job method of development for new employees. Orientation can be:
- Formal
    - Example: all-day mandatory training session.
- Informal
    - Example: one-on-one meeting with a manager for a short period of time.

The most valuable management tool to assist in the orientation process, although not mandatory, is the employee handbook, which details policies and procedures of the organization in addition to serving as an introduction of the new hire to the existing company culture. HR managers plays a key role in developing employee handbooks for an organization as they are fully aware of policies that are required to be included by law, e.g. sexual harassment policy. Studies have found that orientation training is beneficial for multiple reasons, such as:
- Less turnover
- More productivity
- Better morale
- Lower recruitment and training costs
- Reduction of anxiety

HR plays a large role in orientation programs. Typical information covered in these programs are:
- Information about the conditions of employment
- Pay
- Benefits
- Other areas that are not managed by the supervisor

CAREER PLANNING

Human resource planning helps management to develop career paths within their company.

- A **career path** is a succession of linked jobs that prepares the worker for advancement to the next job in the chain. There are two types of career paths:
  - o **Vertical career paths** are hierarchical in nature and consist of interdependent sequential jobs.
  - o **Horizontal career paths** are not sequentially interdependent but each of the jobs in the arrangement must be completed before one can advance to the next higher level.
  - o Jobs within an organization may or may not be part of a career path.
- Workers move through the career path at different speeds:
  - o **Fast tracking** is when an individual advances to the next level in the minimum time required in their current position.
  - o **Career plateauing** is when an individual stops advancing before reaching the highest level.
    - ▪ It is not necessarily a failed effort because not everyone is promoted to the top position.
    - ▪ Many common staff career paths are not designed to lead to the top of the organizational hierarchy.

PRINCIPLES OF LEARNING

When making changes for an organization many companies have chosen to become more of a **learning organization**:

- Is participatory in problem solving, improving, and increasing capabilities.
- Celebrates risks taken in the interest of the organization.
- Values team building and communication and collaboration across departments.
- Empowers the employee to use creativity and freedom of resources.
- Believes in open information so the employees are aware of all sides of an issue or concern before addressing it.

TRAINING PROGRAMS AND METHODS

Human Resource Management is designed to aid managers in helping their employees to develop key skills for better performing their jobs. **Training** generally applies to learning short-term skills. Selection of training and development methods should be tailored to meet individual needs based on the present stage of the worker's career and the career path that they are on. Training can be performed "on-the-job" or "off-the-job," depending on the specific developmental needs of the company and individuals within the organization. Methods of development typically have three purposes:

- Increase job knowledge
- Improve organizational understanding
- Improve interpersonal skills

"On the job" methods of development include:

- Orientation
- Apprenticeship
  - Allows a person to study under a skilled tradesperson at a lower pay rate.
- On the job rotation
  - Allow employees to gain experience in different positions within the organization.
- Coaching
  - Frequent on the job method where managers counsel the subordinates.
  - Performance appraisals are a form of formal coaching.
- Departmental meetings
  - Useful for the development of employee presentation skills.
- Company courses
  - Useful for a shared educational experience with the goal of assuming new or more duties within the organization.
- Various educational programs sponsored by the relationship between a school and the organization:
  - Internships
  - Residencies
  - Assistantships
  - Clerkships
  - Fellowships

"Off the job" methods of development include:
- Off-site seminars
  - Usually sponsored as a learning experience or the chance to network with other professionals in the industry.
- Tuition assistance/reimbursement
  - Job related courses in order to make the worker more valuable to the organization.

DEVELOPMENT PROGRAMS

Development typically applies to learning long-term skills. In order for an organization to compete in any industry they must invest in human capital. To encourage employees to enhance their skills some companies focus on skill development and attach pay acquiring new knowledge or skills (**skill-based pay**). Sometimes organizations use **development assignments** that encourage teamwork and knowledge transfer among the employees.

PART V PERFORMANCE APPRAISALS

Part V accounts for approximately ten percent of the test. This section will cover:

- Reasons for performance evaluation
- Techniques
- Problems

REASONS FOR PERFORMANCE EVALUATION

There are several reasons for performance appraisals that can be characterized by either administrative or developmental. The administrative reasons include:

- Documentation of personnel decisions
- Determination of promotional candidates
- Determination of transfers and reassignments
- Identification of weak performance
- Decision to retain or terminate
- Decide on layoffs
- Validate selection criteria
- Meet legal requirements
- Evaluation of training programs and progress
- Personnel planning
- Reward and compensation decision making

The developmental reasons include:

- Provide feedback for performance
- Identify the individual strength and weaknesses
- Recognize performance
- Assist in identifying goals
- Evaluation of goal achievement
- Identification of training needs
- Determination of organizational training needs
- Reinforcing authoritative structure
- Allowing employees to voice concerns
- Improve the communication within the organization
- Provides a form for help

TECHNIQUES

Developing an effective appraisal program is a collaborative effort between HR and organizational management. When employees are able to participate in the development of a performance appraisal system they are more likely to accept the system. Before an appraisal is done the performance standards should be clearly defined. There are four basic types of performance standards:

- Strategic relevance
    - The standards should relate to the aligned with the eventual goals of an organization.
- Criterion deficiency
    - The standards should capture the range of employee's responsibilities.
    - If the employee is only rated on a single criterion of their job, then the standard is not adequately gauging performance.
- Criterion contamination
    - Rating based on factors outside the employee's control.
- Reliability
    - Consistency of a standard that individuals can maintain over time.

It is important to remember that performance appraisals are used for HR decisions; therefore the data collected must be compliant with the law. Some general guidelines for compliance are:

- Performance ratings should be job related with standards developed from job analysis.
- Job standards must be provided in writing to the employee prior to the appraisal.
- The manager rating the employee must have been able to observe the behavior they are rating.
- Supervisors should be trained in filling out the appraisal form.
- An appeal procedure should be established.

There are several people that can perform an appraisal.

- Manager/supervisor appraisal
  - Traditional approach to performance appraisals.
  - Usually reviewed by management one level higher.
- Self-appraisal
  - Sometimes those getting evaluated are asked to evaluate their selves on a self-appraisal form.
  - This encourages the employee to consider their strengths and weaknesses.
  - Criticism exists for this method because a self-rater will evaluate himself or herself overly favorable.
  - This type of appraisal is best used for developmental purposes.
- Subordinate appraisal
  - Performance appraisal by an employee of their superior.
  - Typically used for developmental purposes.
  - Usually evaluated on:
    - Leadership
    - Oral communication
    - Delegation of authority
    - Coordination of team efforts
    - Interest in subordinates
- Peer appraisals
  - Performance appraisal done by fellow employees.
  - Usually the manager combines them into a single profile for use.
  - While peer appraisals may be the most accurate they have not been used often for a variety of reasons including:
    - Popularity contest
    - Managers do not want to give up control of the appraisal process
    - Those that get poor ratings may retaliate against their peers
    - Peers can rely on stereotypes
  - When peers are competing for bonuses and positions this rating system is not advisable.

- Team appraisals
  - Performance appraisals that recognize team accomplishment instead of individual performance.
  - Usually companies with a strong TQM emphasis will be the ones to use this method.
- Customer appraisal
  - Performance appraisal that seeks evaluation from external and internal customers.
- 360- degree appraisal
  - The combination of various appraisal systems to give the employee and manager the best view into the performance.
  - There are some significant advantages to this appraisal system such as:
    - Comprehensive
    - Quality of information
    - Lessens bias and subjectivity from a single rater
    - Feedback may increase self-development
  - This appraisal system is not without drawbacks:
    - Complexity
    - Can cause resentment
    - Conflicting opinions
    - Employees work together to game the system for over or under inflated marks.
    - Appraisers are not accountable when the feedback is anonymous.
  - Some safeguards necessary for this system are:
    - Assure anonymity
    - Makes respondents accountable
    - Prevent invalid responses
    - Use statistical procedures
    - Indentify biases

Often times any appraisal system fails because the appraiser is not well trained in the process. Appraisers should be trained in the following:
- Establishing an appraisal plan
  - Explanation of the appraisal system
  - Purpose of the system

- Elimination of rater error
  - **Distributional errors** (involves a group of ratings given to various employees)
    - **Error of central tendency** is the reluctance of a rater to give really high or low marks.
    - **Error of leniency or strictness** is where the appraiser gives their employees unusually high or low marks.
  - **Temporal errors** (biased based on how the information is selected, evaluated, or organized)
    - **Recency error** is when the evaluation is based upon the employee's most recent behavior.
    - **Contrast error** is when the employee is compared to someone previously rated and not independently.
    - **Similar to me error** is when the appraiser inflates the evaluation because of mutual connection.
- Feedback training
  - A training program should be provided to the appraisers to cover basic feedback areas, including:
    - Communication
    - Diagnosing root causes
    - Setting goals and objectives

PERFORMANCE APPRAISAL METHODS

There are three basic methods of performance appraisals:

- **Trait methods** measure the extent which someone has characteristics (e.g. reliability, creativity, leadership). They are relatively inexpensive, provide meaningful data, and are easy to use. However, they have high potential for errors, are not geared toward employee counseling, and are not useful in allocating rewards or promotions.
  - **Graphic rating scale**
    - Employee is rated based on having certain characteristics.

- o **Mixed-standard scale**
  - Rating based on comparison (equal, better, or worse) than a standard.
- o **Forced-choice**
  - Requires the rater to choose from statements that best describe the employee's output.
- o **Essay**
  - Requires the rater to describe the employee's performance in a statement.
  - Fairly subjective and reliant on the manager's ability to write effective statements.
- **Behavioral methods** identify the actions that should or should not be seen on the job. This rating system is typically used for developmental feedback. Some advantages to behavioral methods are that they are specific, acceptable to employees and supervisors, useful for feedback, and are fair when making reward and promotion decisions. However, they are time-consuming to develop and use and are susceptible to rating errors.
  - o **Critical incident**
    - Unusual event that identifies superior or inferior performance by the employee.
    - Since the best and worst are discussed individually some employee's refer to this method as the "little black book".
  - o **Behavior checklist**
    - The rater checks statements on a list that he/she believes are characteristic of the employee.
  - o **Behaviorally anchored rating scale (BARS)**
    - Consists of vertical scales for each dimension of the employee's performance.
    - Labor intensive to develop and keep relevant.
  - o **Behavior observation scales (BOS)**
    - Measures the frequency of observed behavior.
- **Results methods** focus on the employee's accomplishments. Results methods are less subjective, acceptable for employees and supervisors, link individual

performance with organizational goals, encourage goal setting, and are good for reward and promotion decisions. However, they are time consuming, can encourage short-term goals only, and can be susceptible to contaminated criteria.

- o **Productivity**
  - Can directly align employees with organizational goals.
  - Evaluation based on profits, sales, etc.
  - Can encourage a feeling of whatever gets measured gets done and other tasks are ignored.
- o **Management by objectives (MBO)**
  - Rates performance on employee achievement of goals set by the manager and the employee.
  - Some guidelines that are helpful in providing MBO are:
    - Managers and employees must be willing to establish the goals together.
    - Objectives should be quantifiable and both long and short term.
    - Expected results must be under the employee's control.
    - Goals should be consistent for each level.
    - Specific timelines should be set, reviewed, and evaluated.
- o **Balanced scorecard (BSC)** helps manager translate measurement framework from strategic to operational goals.
  - Part of the value of a BSC is to show the employee how their actions affect the organization as a whole.
  - Some guidelines for the BSC are:
    - Translate the strategic objectives to clear ones.
    - Attach measurements for each objective.

- Cascade the scorecards to the front line.
- Provide performance feedback.
- Empower employees to make improvements.
- Reassess strategies.

TYPES OF APPRAISAL INTERVIEWS

There are three general types of appraisal interviews:
- Tell and sell
  - Attempt to persuade the employee to alter behavior.
  - Supervisor uses motivational incentives.
- Tell and listen
  - Supervisor communicates the strong and weak points of the employee's performance during the first portion of the interview.
  - The second portion of the interview the supervisor listens to the employee's feelings about the appraisal. By allowing an employee to release frustrations they can better cope with their feelings.
- Problem solving
  - A step beyond tell and sell this stimulates growth of the employee.
  - Employee discusses problems, needs, innovations, satisfactions, and dissatisfactions since last appraisal.

CONDUCTING THE INTERVIEW

Typical guidelines of a successful appraisal interview are:
- Ask for a self-assessment
  - The employee starts thinking about their performance and discussion of the appraisal.
- Invite participation
  - As a general rule the rater should spend about 1/3 of the time talking and the rest listening.
- Express appreciation
  - Starting the interview with what they have done well will help people listen better.
- Minimize criticism
  - When criticizing make it constructive.
  - Consider if the criticism is really necessary (the employee will likely be angry and frustrated after).

- Change the behavior, not the person
  - Stress behavioral issues and how to fix them; do not suggest personality changes (those are difficult).
- Focus on problem solving
  - Do not stress who is at fault for an issue, work on the solution to the problem.
- Be supportive
  - The manager should ask and be willing to help the employee overcome obstacles.
- Establish goals
  - Specific and measurable
    - Expressed in quantitative terms if possible.
    - Avoid vague immeasurable goals.
  - Covers key results
    - Measure what will mean most to a company.
  - Challenging and realistic
    - Goals should be difficult to attain but not unrealistic (to avoid morale issues).
    - **Stretch goals** are extremely hard but not impossible to reach.
  - Defined time period
    - The time period of which a goal is expected should be outlined.
  - Linked to a reward
    - Rewards give meaning to attaining a goal.
- Follow up
  - Feedback should be ongoing, not just during the performance review season.

Formal appraisal programs sometimes fail for various reasons, including:

- Poor preparation by the manager.
- No clear objectives to meet during the period.
- Manager may not have all of the information or observe the performance that is to be rated.
- Inconsistent rating among management.
- Rating on personality not performance.
- The **halo effect**
  o Employee is given the same grade on all dimensions based on a few attributes.
- The **contrast effect**
  o Employee is given an evaluation based on being compared to someone previously evaluated.
- Stereotyping
  o Judging based on a few characteristics.
- Time-span is either too short or long.
- Overly emphasizing uncharacteristic performance.
- Inflated ratings so managers do not have to deal with poor performance.
- Subjective language written in appraisal.
- Organizational politics or personal relationships clouding judgment.
- No thorough discussion of issues with performance.
- Untrained manager giving feedback.
- No follow up or coaching after evaluation.
- Managers feel little benefit will come from the effort.
- Managers do not like confrontation or face-to-face interviews of appraisal.

IMPROVING PERFORMANCE

Sometimes during a performance interview ways to improve performance are identified. Performance can typically be traced back to:

- Motivation
  o Career ambition
  o Employee conflict
  o Frustration
  o Fairness
  o Goals

- Environment
    - Equipment
    - Job design
    - Economic conditions
    - Union
    - Rules and policies
    - Management support
    - Laws and regulations
- Ability
    - Technical skills
    - Interpersonal skills
    - Communication skills
    - Analytical skills
    - Problem-solving skills
    - Physical limitations

Once the reason for poor performance is identified the manager and employee can work on a corrective plan together. Whether it is more training, a transfer, or removal from the organization.

Part VI accounts for approximately fifteen percent of the test. This section will cover:

- Job evaluation
- Wage and salary administration
- Compensation systems
- Benefits

JOB EVALUATION

Job evaluation is the method that determines the relative worth of jobs in order to establish which jobs should be paid more within the organization. There are four basic methods of job evaluation:

- **Job ranking system**
    o This is the oldest and simplest that is based on grouping the jobs based on their relative worth to one another.
    o The outcome is not a precise method of the job's worth and can really only be used on a small number of jobs.
- **Job classification system**
    o Jobs are classified in groups of predetermined wage grades based on responsibilities, skills, and abilities.
        ▪ This is what the federal government uses.
- **Point system**
    o Quantitative job evaluation that determines the value based on points assigned to it.
    o This method takes the development and use of a point manual.
- **Factor comparison system**
    o Evaluation based on factor-by-factor of development and comparison.
    o Compared against the key jobs within the organization. The key jobs are:
        ▪ Important to employees and organization
        ▪ Vary in requirements
        ▪ Have stable job content
        ▪ Used in salary surveys for wages

Job evaluation for management positions are more difficult to evaluate and involve some skills not found at the lower levels of the organization. One method of evaluation of a management

47

position is called the **Hay profile method**. This method evaluates the position based on:
- Knowledge
- Mental activity
- Accountability

The jobs are then ranked based on the point values of each of these factors.

WAGE AND SALARY ADMINISTRATION

While job evaluation is important in knowing the internal equity of the jobs, the wage-rate determination is identified through several tools.

- **Wage and salary survey**
  - This is a survey of the wages paid to employees with similar skill sets in a labor market.
  - The labor market is the area which employers would obtain their resources.
  - The Bureau of Labor Statistics publishes a reliable wage and salary survey.
  - Wage curve
    - The curve in the scattergram that identifies the worth of jobs and wages.
  - Pay grades
    - Groups of jobs within a class that are paid the same (the federal government uses pay grades).
- **Competence based pay**
  - Pay based on the employee's skills and increased job knowledge.
  - Also called skilled based or knowledge based pay.
- **Broadbanding**
  - Collapses traditional salary grades into a few wide bands.
  - Banding helps eliminate obsession with grades and gives management an enhanced ability to reward on performance.

Wages are determined in a variety of ways:
- Internal factors
  - Wage rates based on the employer's ability to pay and the relative worth of the job to the organization.
- External factors
  - Wage rates in labor market, cost of living, collective bargaining (if unionized), and laws.
  - The cost of living is based on the **consumer price index (CPI)** that measures the average prices products and services over time.

COMPENSATION SYSTEMS

Compensation systems are evaluated to determine if they are useful in advancing the organizational goals (**value-added compensation**). The basic goals of a compensation system are to:
- Reward performance
- Remain competitive
- Maintain salary equity
- Tie organizational goals to future performance
- Attract new employees
- Control compensation budget
- Reduce undesired turnover

There are various compensation systems for organizations including:
- **Pay for performance standard** compensation is tied to a reward for effort and performance.
  - Includes merit-based pay, bonuses, salary commissions, job and pay banding, team/group incentives, and gain-sharing programs.
  - To reduce problems within the environment pay should be equitable to contributions.
  - **Pay equity** is how the employee perceives his/her compensation relative to others within the organization.
  - **Pay secrecy** usually breeds mistrust within the workplace.
    - It is a fairly excepted practice in the private industry.

There are several ways employees are compensated, they are:
- **Hourly**
  - Work is paid by the hour.
- **Piecework**
  - Work is paid according to the number of units produced.
- **Salary**
  - Work is paid the same each pay period regardless of hours worked.

BENEFITS - MANDATORY AND VOLUNTARY

The typical reasons for employee benefits are:
- Improve morale
- Meet safety and health requirements
- Attract employees
- Reduce turnover
- Be competitive

Before introducing new benefits the employer should consult employees on whether it is desired. Benefit programs should be nimble enough to meet the needs of a diverse workforce. One of the ways that an employer can meet the needs of many is through the flexible benefit plans (cafeteria plans). **Cafeteria plans** let the employee choose the benefits that are best suited to their personal needs and situation. Cafeteria plans have several advantages:
- Tailored
- Nimble
- Employees self educate
- Employers limit costs by allowing the employee to buy up to a maximum limit.
- Employers are able to recruit and retain an attractive workforce.

However, there are some drawbacks to the cafeteria plans:
- Employee benefit selections affect cost.
- There are added costs to maintain a cafeteria plan.
- Employees can choose benefits that cost the employer more than a typical plan.

There are two types of benefits that employers provide:
- Mandatory (those required by law)
  - Social security insurance
    - Established by the 1935 Social Security Act.

50

- Protects individuals against loss of earnings due to retirement, unemployment, disability, or dependents of the death of a worker.
- To be eligible an employee must have participated in the program (most workers do).
- It is supported by taxes against the employee (which are matched by the employer).
- To fully-qualify for the old-age insurance an employee must reach retirement age (which varies based on when the person was born), earn forty credits (four a year for ten years).
- The amount paid is based on how much the individual earned with adjustments for inflation.
- Social security benefits can be collected if the worker is too disabled to seek gainful employment.
    - The disability must be longer than six months.
    - The disability should expect to last longer than twelve months, or plan to result in death.
- Survivor's insurance benefits are like a life insurance paid to the deceased person's family.
  - Unemployment insurance
    - Unemployment insurance provides a weekly stipend (for those covered under the Social Security Act) for the duration of 26 weeks to individuals who lose a job and are not found to be at fault.
    - In the majority of the states, there are some conditions that will disqualify someone from collecting unemployment insurance compensation, specifically voluntarily quitting one's job without good cause and termination as a result of misconduct.
    - Additionally, unemployment insurance can be revoked at any time during the 26-week period if the unemployed individual refuses

suitable work or if the individual does not actively seek work.
- o Workers compensation insurance
  - ▪ Workers compensation insurance is mandatory in all fifty states.
  - ▪ Employers pay into a no-fault insurance system that compensates employees for medical expenses associated with job-related illness or injury.
  - ▪ In the event that an individual suffers a job-related death, the benefit is paid to the family of the deceased worker.
- o Consolidated Omnibus Budget Reconciliation Act (COBRA)
  - ▪ Employers must make health coverage (at the same rate the employer would pay) available to employees, spouses, and dependents upon termination of employment, death, or divorce.
  - ▪ The coverage must be offered between 18 and 36 months depending on the situation.
- o Older Workers Benefit Protection Act (OWBPA)
  - ▪ Passed by Congress in 1990 seeks to protect older workers from discrimination.
- • Voluntary
  - o Health insurance
    - ▪ Health insurance benefits get the most attention from employees.
    - ▪ Covers anything from medical, surgical, hospital, prescription, mental health, optical, and dental.
    - ▪ **Health Maintenance Organizations (HMO)**
      - • Organization of healthcare professionals that provide services on a prepaid basis.
      - • Lowers health costs for employee and employer.
      - • Seen as lower quality to the employee.
    - ▪ **Preferred Provider Organization (PPO)**

- Group of healthcare providers that guarantee lower healthcare costs to the employer.
- Employees have greater flexibility in choosing their medical provider.
- Seen as a higher quality medical plan to the employee.
  - **Medical savings account (MSA)**
    - Medical insurance plan that the employer contributes to meet the needs of the individual's medical needs (insurance, etc).
  - **Health Insurance Portability and Accountability Act (HIPAA)**
    - After twelve months worked at an employer with health insurance that worker can transfer to another employer with no regard to pre-existing conditions.
- Long-term disability (LTD) insurance
  - Pays for nursing homes and medical-related costs to old age and illness.
- **Supplemental unemployment benefits (SUBS)**
  - An employer creates a fund for laid off employees to draw from on top of the unemployment benefits.
- Life insurance
  - Usually allows employees to purchase significant benefits at minimal charges.
- Prerequisites and services
  - Pension contributions
  - Legal assistance
  - Tuition assistance
  - Day care provision
  - Paid time off (sick, vacation, maternity, holiday, paternity, severance, and personal)
- **Employee assistance programs (EAP)**
  - Services provided for workers to deal with problems that interfere with how they do their jobs.
  - Counseling

- Family
- Marriage
- Mental health
■ Child and elder care
- Financial assistance
- Alternative work schedules
- Family leave
- Dependent care spending account
o Retirement programs
■ Pension plans
- Federal regulations of pension plans
  o It is not required for an employer to provide a pension plan, but if they do they must follow the regulations.
  o Requires certification by actuary every three years.
  o States that all plans must have **vesting** (guarantee of benefits) be clearly laid out.
- **Contributory**
  o Employee and employer fund pensions.
- **Noncontributory**
  o Only employer funds pensions.
- **Defined benefit plan**
  o The amount is specific.

- **Defined contribution plan**
  - Amount of benefits are based on how much is in their account at time of retirement.
- **401(k) savings**
  - Today it is the main source of retirement funds.
  - Some employers will match contributions to a certain percentage.
- **Cash balance pension plans**
  - Employer contributes percentage of employer pay and the account earns interest.
  - Upon leaving employer the amount can be rolled into an IRA.
- To avoid layoffs some employers offer the silver handshake to older workers.
  - The **silver handshake** is an early-retirement incentive in the form of a cash bonus or increased pension.
- Other services
  - Food
    - Vending machines, cafeterias, lunch trucks, catering
  - Onsite health services
    - Flu shots, nurse office
  - Legal help
    - Access or comprehensive plans
  - Financial planning
  - Housing and moving expenses
  - Transportation pooling
  - Purchasing assistance
    - Discounts through retailers
  - Credit unions
  - Recreational and social services
  - Awards

PART VII SAFETY AND HEALTH

Part VII accounts for approximately five percent of the test. This section will cover:

- Occupational accidents and illness
- Quality of work life
- Workplace security

OCCUPATIONAL ACCIDENTS AND ILLNESS

Congress passed the Occupational Safety and Health Act (OSHA) in 1970 to attempt to reduce workplace injuries and illnesses. The four major categories that are within OSHA's area of responsibility are:

- General industry
- Maritime
- Construction
- Agriculture

OSHA covers the workplace, machinery, equipment, power sources, processing, protective clothing, and administrative requirements. The Secretary of Labor has the authority to do workplace inspections and give citations for violations. There are four levels of inspections for OSHA:

- First level
  - o Inspect imminent danger situations.
- Second level
  - o Investigate catastrophes, fatalities, and accidents that resulted in injury of five or more employees.
- Third level
  - o Investigate employee complaints of violations.
- Fourth level
  - o Special emphasis inspections aimed at high-hazard industries.

Citations can either be given immediately or mailed to the employer after the inspection. The violations must be posted for three days or until the violation is corrected (whichever is longer). OSHA can give the following citations and penalties:

- Other than serious
  - o Violation of job safety but unlikely to cause death.
  - o Up to $7000 per violation.

- Serious
  - Violation with substantial probability of death or serious harm.
  - Up to $7000 per violation.
- Willful
  - Violation that the employer intentionally commits or shows plain indifference.
  - Up to $70000 per violation.
  - If a willful violation results in an employee death OSHA can fine $250000 for an individual or $500000 for a company (or six months prison).

Aside from citing employers for violations OSHA can also help employers identify and correct hazards. OSHA provides:
- Free onsite consultation
  - Government representatives help to identify hazards and how to correct them.
  - No citations are issued in connection with a consultation and it will not trigger an inspection.
- **Voluntary protection program** (VPPs)
  - Programs that encourage employers to go beyond minimum requirements outlined by OSHA.
  - There are three VPPs:
    - Star
    - Merit
    - Demonstration

OSHA gives the employer and employee certain rights and responsibilities:
- Employer
  - Must inform employees of the safety and health requirements of OSHA.
  - Keep records and post an annual summary of work-related injuries and illnesses.
    - From the records comes the incidence rate.
    - The incidence rate is used for making comparisons between work groups within and outside of an organization.
  - Ensure employee's wear protective equipment, and provide safety training.
  - Discipline employees for noncompliance with safety regulations.

- o Under the right-to-know laws employers must notify the employees of any hazardous materials they handle.
  - ▪ The **Material Safety Data Sheets (MSDS)** are documents that contain the main information about hazardous chemicals.
- Employee
  - o Comply with safety regulations.
  - o Report hazardous conditions.
  - o Follow employer health rules and regulations.
  - o Workers have a right to a safe and healthy workplace without being punished.
  - o Employees have a right to know about any hazardous chemicals they handle.

When accidents do occur they are recorded on the **OSHA form 300**. A recordable case is any that causes accidental death, illness, or injury to an employee. Some of the common health hazards that exist in the workplace today are:

- Chemical
  - o Many are harmful and can remain in the body for years.
  - o All chemicals must be labeled with the MSDS and required chemical handling training is provided for the employees.
- Indoor air quality
  - o Due to energy efficiency many buildings are being sealed better, but ventilation suffers.
  - o Four basic ways to overcome a polluted building are:
    - ▪ Eliminate smoking inside
    - ▪ Provide proper ventilation
    - ▪ Maintain ventilation system
    - ▪ Remove sources of pollution
- Computer related injuries
  - o Visual difficulties from monitoring screens
  - o Muscle aches and pains from the sedentary position
  - o Job stress
  - o Cumulative trauma disorders
    - ▪ Injuries involving tendons of fingers, hands, and arms from repeated strain (carpel tunnel syndrome).

- Some tips on resolving computer related injuries are:
  - Computer screen 4 to 9 inches below eye level
  - Monitor in front
  - Adjustable height chair
  - Screen with adjustable brightness
  - Avoid monitor glare
  - Ergonomically designed furniture, keyboards, etc.

QUALITY OF WORK LIFE

Employers should not only improve hazardous conditions but also try to improve lives of their workers, as it is shown to:
- Increase efficiency
- Reduce absenteeism
- Improve morale
- Reduce turnover

Quality of work life can be addressed by:
- Ensuring healthful employees
  - Preemployment exams (including drug testing)
- Alternative health approaches
  - Chiropractic
  - Acupuncture
  - Herbal therapy
- Promoting health and fitness
  - Nutrition lessons
  - Company sports teams
  - Consulting a personal training
- Employee assistance programs (EAP)
  - Dealing with personal crisis
    - Marital, family, or legal matters
    - Usually short term
  - Emotional problems
    - Depression lowers productivity, causes morale and absentee problems.

- o Alcoholism
  - ▪ Classified as a disability under the American with Disabilities Act.
  - ▪ Help should be made available without penalty.
- o Illegal drug use
  - ▪ Reasonable accommodation and enroll in a drug treatment program.
  - ▪ Can be fired if they are under federal requirements.

Employers should help the employee manage stress. Stress is any demand on an individual. There are two types of stress:

- **Eustress**
  - o Positive stress that strives some to accomplish something.
- **Distress**
  - o Harmful stress that accompanies a feeling of insecurity.
  - o The most severe stage of distress is burnout.
    - ▪ **Burnout** causes loss of productivity, frustration, and depression.

Stress coordinates the mobilization of the body to deal with the stress. The fight or flight response is called the alarm reaction. The **alarm reaction** is characterized by increased heart rate, respiration, and elevated levels of adrenaline. Job related stress is caused by:

- High workloads
- Lay offs
- Organizational restructuring
- Global economic conditions
- Disagreements with managers or peers
- Lack of communication
- Responsibility without authority
- Inability to complain
- Discrimination
- Poor working conditions
- Inadequate recognition
- Lack of clear job description
- Hostile environment
- Minor irritations

To deal with stress organizations can:

- Redesign and enrich jobs
- Develop stress management programs
- Clarify the employees role
- Correct physical factors of stress in the workplace

WORKPLACE SECURITY

OSHA has five recommendation of reducing workplace violence:
- Management commitment and employee involvement in preventing violence.
- Analyze workplace to reveal areas of potential violence.
- Prevent violence by creating a safe work place and practice.
- Provide violence prevention training.
- Evaluate violence program effectiveness.

Additionally, employers should carefully screen job applicants through methods such as background checks. There are several warning signs that someone may become violent including:
- Direct or veiled threats
- Performance declining with excessive excuses
- Mood changes
- Preoccupation with weapons
- Sabotage
- Fascination with violent stories
- Antisocial behavior
- Aggressive behavior
- Substance abuse
- Violence against a family member

Since September 11, 2001 terrorism has been an ongoing threat. At minimum workplaces should know:
- Escape route
- Emergency equipment
- Special assistance for the disabled
- Where to meet

PART VIII EMPLOYEE RIGHTS AND DISCIPLINE

Part VIII accounts for approximately five percent of the test.

EMPLOYEE RIGHTS

Employee rights guarantee the fair treatment from employers and outline the right to employee privacy. While employers must respect their employees' rights, they must also balance responsibilities to guarantee quality goods and services to their consumers. Employers must exercise reasonable care in hiring, training, and assigning employees. If an employer fails to provide reasonable care and an injury results the employer can be liable. The general rule of employees and employers is employment at will. **Employment-at-will** basically is the right for an employer to terminate an employee for any or no reason and the employee to resign for the same. The Fourth and Fifth Amendment spells out some Constitutional rights for public sector employees. There are three basic exceptions to the **employment-at-will** principle:

- Violation of public policy
    - Employee refuses to commit a crime.
    - Reports criminal activity to the government (**whistleblowing**).
    - Exercising employment rights.
- Implied contract
    - Terminated after employers promise (implied or expressed) that they would have job security.
    - Courting someone from another company with better wages, then not providing them.
- Implied covenant
    - Lack of good faith and fair dealing of employer is suggested.
    - Employer violates covenant and can be responsible for damages.

Constructive discharge is when an employer makes work life so difficult for the employee that they have no choice but to resign. The employer can be held liable for the resignation in this case.

Employers have some rights to investigate the persons working for them, and employees should expect less privacy in the workplace than at home.

- Drug testing
    - The ADA covers recovering addicts but not people currently using illegal drugs.
    - Urinalysis is the most common form of testing but other methods are blood and hair samples.
    - Employers have several reasons to test for drugs:
        - Pre-employment
        - Safety-sensitive positions (to avoid endangerment of self or others)
        - Security-sensitive (handling confidential materials)
        - Reasonable suspicion
        - Post-accident (to determine if drugs played a role)
        - Return-to-duty (after rehabilitation)
        - Follow-up (to recheck after a failed test)
        - Random
- Employee search and surveillance
    - Policy should be widely publicized.
    - Applied in a reasonable manner.
    - When possible, conducted in private.
    - Employer should try to gain consent prior to search.
    - Conducted humanely and discreetly.
    - Penalty for noncompliance should be specific.
- Access to personnel files
    - Usually contains performance appraisals, salary notices, investigative reports, credit checks, criminal records, test scores, and family data.
    - Medical information cannot be kept in the same file as the other personnel information.
    - About half the states have laws that grant them the right to inspect their own personnel files.
- Email/Internet and voice mail privacy
    - Typically employers have the right to monitor their own equipment (including email and Internet usage).

- o Employees can be terminated for inappropriate Internet, voice mail, and email usage.
  - o Employers should be specific of how email and Internet are monitored and how they should be used.
- Employee conduct outside the workplace
  - o Employers who want to discipline their worker due to outside conduct must establish a clear relationship to workplace impact.

DISCIPLINE POLICIES AND PROCEDURES

Discipline has three meanings:
- Treatment that punishes.
- Orderly behavior in an organization.
- Training that corrects undesirable behavior and develops self-control.

If a supervisor fails to take action against a person that is violating the rules of the workplace they are sending the message that their behavior is satisfactory. The most common reasons that a supervisor does nothing about poor behavior are:
- No documentation of earlier actions.
- Supervisor does not believe management will support them.
- Supervisor uncertain of facts or situation.
- Supervisor stays consistent in not punishing certain infractions.
- Supervisor wants to be liked.

The **hot-stove approach** to discipline is that, like a hot stove, it is effective, consistent, and applied to all equally. During the investigation of employee misconduct there are several steps:
- Documentation of misconduct
  - o Date/time
  - o Problem
  - o Consequences
  - o Prior discussions about problem
  - o Action to be taken and improvement expected
  - o Consequences if action is not taken
  - o Employee reaction
  - o Names of witnesses (if needed)
- Investigative interview
  - o Before action is taken an interview should be done so the employee is aware of their offense.

- It should be unbiased and give the employee an opportunity to give their side.
- An investigative interview should be done privately.

There are two main approaches to discipline:
- Progressive
  - Corrective measures by increasing degrees.
  - Uses only enough discipline to correct the problem.
  - Most commonly used.
  - Typically four steps:
    - Oral warning
    - Written warning
    - Suspension without pay
    - Discharge
- Positive
  - Focuses on the early correction of employee misconduct.
  - Typically three steps:
    - Conference between employee and supervisor to find a solution to the problem (supervisor does not reprimand or threaten with more disciplinary action).
      - Supervisors may document the conference, but unless the action happens again it will not be stored in a personnel file.
    - Second conference to determine why solution agreed upon did not work.
      - Written reminder given to the employee.
    - Decision-making leave (paid leave)
      - Duration is one day with the purpose of coming back with a decision of whether the employee wishes to continue working for the employer.
      - Come back with a total commitment to correction or prepare to leave the organization.

Additionally there are alternative dispute resolution procedures. An **alternative resolution procedure** (ARD) are different types of employee complaint resolution procedures.
- Step-review system

- o Resolution by successive higher levels of management.
- Peer-review system
  - o Group of employee and management representatives that act as a jury and render a decision.
- Open-door policy
  - o Policy of settling disputes with various levels of management above the supervisor.
- Ombudsman system
  - o Designated individual whom employees can seek counsel and resolution.
- Mediation
  - o Neutral party hears both sides and renders compromise.

Part IX accounts for approximately fifteen percent of the test. This section will cover:

- Equal employment opportunity laws
- Compensation and benefits related
- Health, safety and employee rights laws
- Union laws

EQUAL EMPLOYMENT OPPORTUNITY LAWS

Equal Employment Opportunity laws are passed to ensure **protected classes** (minorities in the workplace) have equal opportunity to employment. Some of the major federal laws are:

- **Title VII of Civil Rights Act of 1964 (amended in 1972, 1991, and 1994)**
  - Broadest and most significant law affecting employment opportunity rights.
  - No discrimination based on race, color, religion, sex, or nationality.
  - Only suitable defense against discrimination is a **Bona Fide Occupational Qualification** (BFOQ) (age, religion, sex, or nationality is an actual qualification for the job). BFOQ does NOT cover race or color.
    - **Business necessity** is a work related practice for the efficient operation of an organization and is considered a legal defense under the Civil Rights Act.
- **Age Discrimination in Employment Act of 1967 (amended in 1986 and 1990)**
  - No discrimination based on age of person's over 40 (unless age is a specific qualification).
  - No pressuring for an older person to take retirement.
  - No terminating only older employees when downsizing.
  - No selection of younger candidates over older better-qualified ones.
- **Equal Employment Opportunity Act of 1972**

- o Extended Title VII to government workers and others.
- **Vocational Rehabilitation Act (1973)**
  - o Federal employers with contracts over $2,500 must take action to hire disabled individuals.
  - o However, they are not required to hire someone that is under-qualified just because they are disabled.
  - o **Disabled** is indentified by:
    - Person with a mental or physical impairment that limits activities.
    - Impairment is recorded.
    - Person is regarded as having the impairment.
- **Pregnancy Discrimination Act of 1978**
  - o No discrimination based on pregnancy, childbirth, and related conditions.
- **Americans with Disabilities Act (ADA) of 1990**
  - o Employers cannot discriminate against people with physical or mental disabilities.
  - o Employers must make **reasonable accommodations** (adjust without undue hardship working conditions and schedules) for people with disabilities or religious preferences.
- **Civil Rights Act of 1991**
  - o Discriminated against employees can seek punitive damages.
- **Uniformed Services Employment and Reemployment Rights Act of 1994**
  - o Jobs are protected for those that go on short military service.
- **Executive Order 11246**
  - o Federal agencies and government contractors (holding contracts valued at $10,000 or more) must comply with antidiscrimination practices of this executive order.
  - o No discrimination based on race, color, religion, sex, or national origin on all employment activities.

- o This executive order created the Office of Federal Contract Compliance Programs (OFCCP) to enforce compliance.
- **Immigration Reform and Control Act of 1986**
  - o Used to control the hiring, recruiting, or referring of people not eligible to work in the United States.
  - o To comply with the act employers must:
    - Have employees fill out the form I-9.
    - Check employees' identity.
    - Complete the employer's section of the I-9.
    - Retain I-9 for three years (at least).
    - Present the I-9 to government if requested.
- **EEO-1 Report**
  - o Companies with 100 or more employees must fill out the employer information report annually to determine the workforce composition.

SEXUAL HARASSMENT

As barriers between people disappear, sexual harassment has become more common. There are varying levels of sexual harassment:
- **Generalized**
  - o Sexual remarks or actions not targeted at a specific individual.
- **Inappropriate**
  - o Nonthreatening, but causes co-worker discomfort.
- **Solicitation with reward**
  - o Potential for criminal prosecution for soliciting sexual acts.
- **Coercion with threat**
  - o Threat of power (recommendations, performance evaluations, etc.) in order to convince someone to engage in sexual activity.
- **Sexual crimes**
  - o Highest level and would result in a punishable act under the law.

Additionally, the Equal Employment Opportunity recognizes two forms of sexual harassment.
- **Quid pro quo harassment**
  - o Harassment based on employment decisions.
  - o Economic or position consequence for noncompliance.

- **Hostile environment**
  - Creates an uncomfortable environment that interferes with job performance.
  - Obscenity, nudity, dirty jokes, etc. are tied to a hostile environment.

SIGNIFICANT COURT CASES

- *Griggs v Duke Power Company* (1971)
  - Discrimination does not have to be overt or intentional.
  - Employment practices must be job related.
- *Albermarle Paper Company v Moody (*1975)
  - Strengthened *Griggs* principles
  - Testing must be directly related to job relatedness.
- *Wards Cove Packing Co. v Atonio* (1989)
  - Statistical disparity does not by itself prove discrimination

PROCESSING CHARGES

The Equal Employment Opportunity Commission (EEOC) is responsible for investigating charges of discrimination. If a person believes they have been discriminated against, the procedure is as follows:

- Employee fills out a **charge form** (official discrimination complaint to EEOC).
  - Charges are given to employer, state agency, and the EEOC for investigation.
- EEOC investigates the charge and it is either:
  - Dismissed (the individual can still challenge this decision in court).
  - Settled with the company.
  - Or a reasonable cause is found and if the EEOC and the organizational cannot settle within 180 days, then a suit is filed.

Before equal employment opportunity (EEO) laws and affirmative action were introduced to the business world, many people suffered discrimination by the hand of potential employers. As a result of EEO laws and affirmative action programs, the workplace has increasingly become much more diverse than it was in the past. **Workforce diversity** means that the people employed in an organization represent different cultural groups and human qualities. Today's workforce employs a greater number of minorities, as well as older employees, particularly those of the baby-boom generation, or "boomers."

Four approaches to organizational diversity are:

- **Strategic diversity management**
  - o Results of acquisitions and mergers, which in a way is sort of a forced diversification of the workplace.
- **Managing workforce diversity**
  - o Organizations seek to minimize **ethnocentrism** (the belief that one culture is superior to another).
  - o Organizations are moving toward embracing **pluralism** (accommodation of several cultures), and **ethnorelativism** (idea that all cultures are inherently equal).
- **Understanding differences**
  - o **Diversity awareness training** is designed to make people recognize and address their own prejudices.
- **Affirmative action**
  - o Developed in response to the white male domination of the workforce.

COMPENSATION AND BENEFITS RELATED LAWS

There are many compensation and benefits related laws including:

- **Davis-Bacon Act**
  - o Passed in 1931.
  - o Required federal contracts for construction to specify minimum wage of workers.
- **Walsh-Healy Act**
  - o Passed in 1936.
  - o Responsible for:
    - ▪ Prevailing minimum wage in a locality.
    - ▪ Regular working hours identified as eight in a day and forty in a week.

- ▪ Time and a half pay for additional hours.
    - ▪ No employment for convicts and children.
    - ▪ Established standards for safety and sanitation.
- **Fair Labor Standards Act (FLSA) in 1938**
    - o Provides the basic pay structure for workers.
    - o Workers who legally have to be paid according to the Fair Labor Standards Act are referred to as "non-exempt."
    - o Other workers, generally those who hold executive, managerial and professional positions, are not covered by the FLSA, and are referred to as "exempt."
    - o Federal minimum wage is one important term of the law, which secures a basic minimum wage for all non-exempt workers.
    - o Additionally, under FLSA, non-exempt workers are guaranteed overtime pay when hours worked in any given week exceed the standard workweek, which is typically 40 hours per week.
    - o Forbids employment of minors between 16 and 18 in hazardous jobs.
- **Equal Pay Act of 1963**
    - o Passed as an amendment to the Fair Labor Standards Act (FLSA).
    - o No discrimination of pay, benefits, or pension based on gender.
    - o Equal is defined by the same skill, effort, and responsibility.
- **Employee Retirement Income Security Act (ERISA) of 1974**
    - o Main federal legislation responsible for controlling employee benefit and retirement plans.
    - o All decision-making power in regards to employment benefit plans belongs to the federal government.

- **Family and Medical Leave Act (FMLA)**
  - Passed in August of 1993 the Family Medical Leave Act applies to employers with fifty or more employees.
  - Paternal and maternal leave are covered under this act.
  - An employee can take twelve workweeks of unpaid leave (with their jobs reserved for them) under the following conditions:
    - Birth of a child
    - Adoption
    - Care for an immediate family member with a medical condition.
  - Health condition of employee.

The **Occupational Safety and Health Act (OSHA)** of 1970 requires all employers to furnish to each of its employees employment and a place of employment which are free from recognized hazards that are causing or are likely to cause death or serious physical harm in the General Duty Clause. The Secretary of Labor is responsible for setting occupational safety and health standards that employers are required to follow per OSHA. There are three categories of safety and health standards that OSHA requires the Secretary of Labor to issue:

- Establish federal standards
- Establish national consensus standards
- Establish additional standards
    o Some standards are industry-specific but many apply to a wide-range of industries.

The **Worker Adjustment and Retraining Notification (WARN) Act** only affects employers with one hundred or more employees, and requires the employer to give advance notice of at least sixty days when a plant closing or mass layoff is planned. The WARN Act takes into account that there are some instances when circumstances could not possibly have been predicted to give advanced notice.

UNION LAWS

Labor and management relations are important to organizations, government, and individuals. There have been important legislative actions that impact management and labor relations.

- **Wagner Act (National Labor Relations Act)**
    o Passed in 1935 and referred to as the Magna Carta of Labor.
    o Guarantees the right to form labor movements (**unions**) and to choose representation to collectively bargain and strike.
    o Five major "unfair labor practices" were banned by the act.
        ▪ Interference with the formation of a union.
        ▪ Interference with the right to collectively bargain.
        ▪ Encourage or discourage union membership.

- Discrimination based on charges filed under the Wagner Act.
- Refusing to bargain with the union.
  - o The National Labor Relations Board (NLRB) was formed as a result of the Wagner Act in order to supervise labor union and management interactions and led to the new face of Human Resource Management.
  - o Unions responsible for creating closed shop security arrangements that required workers to belong to the proper union before they could obtain work with certain companies.
- **Taft-Hartley Act (Labor Management Relations Act)**
  - o Pro-business act passed in 1947, was enacted to counter the pro-labor Wagner Act, consequently banning unfair practices of labor unions.
    - Coercing workers to bargain through representatives.
    - Barring employment based on union membership and non-paying dues.
    - Striking to force employees to join a union.
  - o Created the Federal Mediation and Conciliation Service (FMCS) to help resolve grievances.
    - Neutral party who communicates with both sides for the purpose of agreement.
  - o Open shops were created as a result of the law giving states the power to pass "right-to-work" laws that prevent workers from being forced to join a union.
  - o The act created several additional procedures including:
    - Established procedures for averting national emergency strikes.
    - Excluded managers from union coverage.
    - Prohibited the closed-shop (union only) jobs.
    - Banned discrimination based on non-union status.

The Taft-Harley Act was modified to include major additions under the Landrum-Griffin Act.

- **Landrum-Griffin Act**

- Passed in 1959 also known as the **Labor-Management Reporting and Disclosure Act**.
- Identified more unfair practices:
  - Ban on organizational picketing.
  - Allowing State Labor relations to decide over disputes that the NLRB did not consider.

OTHER IMPORTANT LEGISLATION TO UNIONS

There are numerous legislative actions that have impacted unions, but the following are some of the most prominent.

- **Clayton Act**
  - Passed in 1914 targeted to labor organizations.
  - No forbidding the existence of a union.
- **Railway Labor Act**
  - Passed in 1926 requiring the employers to collectively bargain with unions.
  - In 1936 it was amended to include airlines.
- **Norris-LaGuardia Act**
  - Passed in 1932.
  - Prohibited federal courts from enforcing "**yellow dog**" contracts (workers had to promise not to join a union or discontinue membership).
  - Barred businesses from stopping the following activities:
    - Joining a union.
    - Striking or refusing to work.
    - Publicizing labor dispute.
    - Providing legal aid to persons in dispute.

Part X Labor Relations

Part X accounts for approximately six percent of the test. This section will cover:

- Unions
- Collective bargaining
- Unionized versus non-unionized work settings

Unions

Labor relations is primarily four stages:
- Workers want collective representation
- Union organizes and campaigns
- Collective negotiations lead to a contractual agreement
- Contract is administered

Why employees unionize

Employee unionize for several reasons including:
- Union shop
    - Some workplaces (where legal) make it a requirement to join the union in order to seek employment.
- Economic
    - If employees believe they can acquire better wages under a union.
- Dissatisfaction with management
    - If employees believe management is being unfair in hiring, promotion, shifts, or other job environmental factors.
- Social and status
    - Ability to socialize with other employees in similar circumstances.

The campaign process

Usually the employees begin organizing. The typical steps to organization are:
- Employee/union contract
    - Investigation of the advantages of unionization
    - Union organizers gather information on the issues employees face and what they hope to get from the union.
- Initial organization meeting

- o Meeting to attract supporters.
- o Identify employees who can help the organizer through campaigning.
- o Establish communication to employees of union progress.
- Formation of committee (in-house)
  - o In-house employees who are willing to lead the campaign.
  - o Employees sign an **authorization card** (statement authorizing union to act as their representative).
- Election petition and voting
  - o If enough employees support the union, then they will seek a government-sponsored election.
  - o Representation petition filed with NLRB who will hold a secret-ballot election to determine if unionizing is really what the employees want.
- Contract negotiations
  - o If union wins the election the NLRB will certify the union as the legal bargaining for the employees.
  - o Management and the union will enter into negotiations for working conditions.

STRUCTURE OF A UNION

There are a few different types of unions:
- Craft unions
  - o Represent skilled craft workers (carpenters, masons, etc.).
- Industrial unions
  - o Represents unskilled and semiskilled worker

In 1955 the American Federation of Labor and the Congress of Industrial Organizations merged to form the AFL-CIO. The AFL-CIO is a group of individual unions who come together for:
- Lobbying
- Organizing efforts of affiliation
- Publicizing union interests
- Resolved disputes between unions

There are two types of unions:
- National
  - o Larger and have major influence over the unions that comprise them.
  - o National unions:
    - ▪ Train leaders

78

- Provide legal assistance
- Lead in political activity
- Educate and hold public relation campaigns
- Disciple union members
- Local
  - Negotiate the local labor agreement
  - Investigate grievances
  - Typically have a president, vice president, secretary/treasure and other committee members.
  - **Union steward** is an important part of the local union; operates as an unpaid union official that represents the employees when dealing with management.

COLLECTIVE BARGAINING

There are four basic steps to the bargaining process:
- Prepare for negotiations
  - Gathering data
  - Forming terms
- Develop strategies
  - Develop compromising limits
  - Consider opponent goals
  - Make plans to strike
- Conduct negotiations
  - Bargain
  - Analyze proposals
  - Resolve proposal
  - Stay within the bargain zone
- Formalize agreement
  - Clarify contractual language
  - Ratify the agreement

If the union and management cannot successfully reach an agreement the union and management have several tactics:
- Union
  - Boycotting (refusing to patronize the employer)
  - Striking (pickets the employer at the business entrances)
    - Usually unions will not violate each other's pickets; therefore this can stop deliveries into the business.
- Management
  - Continue operations despite boycott and strikes.

- During a strike management can legally hire replacement workers.
- Management can do the jobs of the workers during a strike.
- Management can lockout the employees preventing them from working and shutting down its operations.

During extreme cases where the mediation and voluntary compromising process fails they can resolve disputes with an arbitrator. An **arbitrator** is a neutral third party that will make the binding decision between both parties.

LABOR AGREEMENT

Most of the labor agreements are resolved peacefully and the result is a binding document with terms/conditions/ and rules. This documents is a **labor agreement**. If the labor agreement is violated there is a five-step grievance procedure:

- The person speaks to their immediate supervisor (resolution is expected in five working days).
- The union steward speaks to the immediate supervisor (resolution is expected in ten working days).
- The chief steward addresses the issue with the department manager (resolution is expected in fifteen working days).
- The local union president addresses the issue with the VP of industrial relations (resolution is expected in thirty working days).
- If no resolution, then the VP industrial relations manager and the local union president go to arbitration.
  - **Fair representation** (union must represent union and nonunion members equally).

Unionized versus non-unionized work settings

Unions are becoming less common today than in years passed. Unions are doing their best to increase efforts. The most recent focus has been the lowest tier of the economy and the white-collar workers. Management has employed several strategies to try to keep unions out of their workplace:

- Creating competitive wages and benefits.
- Training supervisors on improved human relations skills.
- Establishing formal procedures for complaint resolution.
- Involving employees in decision-making.
- Helping employees grow and develop.
- Making fair HR policies and applying them equally.

PART XI INTERNATIONAL HUMAN RESOURCE
MANAGEMENT

Part XI accounts for approximately four percent of the test. Managers must understand the culture to be able to provide leadership, make decisions, motivate, and control. There are different kinds of international staff including:

- **Expatriates** (or home country nationals) are employees who live and work in a different country than their own.
    o The failure rate is between 25% and 50%.
    o **Repatriation** is the process of an employee coming back to the home country after international assignment.
    o Compensation should provide for:
        ▪ Incentive to leave the U.S.
        ▪ Live like an American while overseas.
            • The **balance sheet approach** is the compensation system that equals American money to foreign money in terms of purchasing power.
        ▪ Facilitate reentry to the U.S.
        ▪ Provide for children's' education.
        ▪ Allow the maintenance of relationships in the U.S.
- **Host-country nationals** are employees who are host country natives.
    o After set up an organization usually shifts to this because it is cheaper, gives a good impression on local governments, and people do not have to adjust to the culture.
- **Third-country nationals** are employees that are not from the host or home country.

Managing in a foreign country brings a unique set of challenges, including:

- Personal challenges
    o Give up any attempt at ethnocentrism (the belief that one's own culture is better than another).
    o Homesickness
    o **Culture shock** (feeling of disorientation and fear from being immersed in a foreign culture).

- Managing
  - Leading
    - If collectivism is high, then leaders should be warm and personal.
    - Some countries disrespect brings dishonor to the entire family.
  - Decision making
    - Depending on the country some cultures sense participatory decision-making as a weakness in the manager.
  - Motivating
    - Some countries find rewards for individuals to be unmotivating.
    - Understand what motivates the employee based on their culture and use it.
  - Controlling
    - Do not control the wrong things. Be careful and pick the battles that are worth fighting.

An organization must be cognizant of the local laws and should be responsive to the cultural and political environments. For those that become global managers training can provide the information and tools they need to be a success.

PART XII CURRENT ISSUES AND TRENDS

Part XII accounts for four percent of the test. This section will cover:

- Workforce diversity
- Human resource information systems
- Changing patterns of work relationships (e.g., virtual office, contingent workers, autonomous work groups)

WORKFORCE DIVERSITY

Before equal employment opportunity (EEO) laws and affirmative action, discrimination was common. As a result of EEO laws and affirmative action programs, the workplace has increasingly become much more diverse than it was in the past. Today's workforce employs a greater number of minorities, as well as older employees. A diverse organization has a strategic advantage over their competitors, especially in the global marketplace, as workers come from a wide-range of backgrounds, and bring fresh and varied insights to the table. Despite EEO laws some barriers within an organization still exist. They are most often referred to as the "**glass ceiling**," and the "**brick wall**."

Four approaches to organizational diversity are:

- Strategic diversity management
  - Strategic diversity management occurs as a result of acquisitions and mergers, which in a way is sort of a forced diversification of the workplace.
- Managing workforce diversity
- Understanding differences
- Affirmative action

The Society for Human Resource Management has generated a list of nine recommendations for executing an effective diversity initiative:

- Executive commitment to diversity.
- Articulate outcomes of diversity.
- Assess climate, needs and issues at the organization.
- Create and maintain open channels of communication with employees.
- Implement diversity taskforce to widen support.
- Develop a mechanism for dealing with systemic changes and procedural problems.

- Design and implement diversity training.
- Evaluate and measure effectiveness of diversity programs.
- Integrate and accountability for diversity programs.

HUMAN RESOURCE INFORMATION SYSTEMS

Human resources information system (HRIS) are systems the provide data for HR control and decision-making. There are three impacts IT has on HR:

- Operational
  - Automating repetitive activities (payroll).
  - Reduces the administrative burden.
- Relational
  - Remote access to other HR systems within the organization.
- Transformational
  - Helps a company move forward on how to go about certain activities.
  - Example is training and beginning to use an IT system.

Some of the major functions of an HR system are:

- Payroll
- Employee data
- Benefits administration
- Compensation planning and management
- Compliance reporting
- Performance management
- Organizational management
- Recruitment and selection
- Retiree administration
- Human resources planning
- Employee training and development
- Employee relations
- Diversity programs

CHANGING PATTERNS OF WORK RELATIONSHIPS

There are several changing patterns in the new working relationships including:

- Virtual office

- o **Virtual teams** have team members that are not logistically close but communicate through technology.
- o **Telecommuting** is the use of personal computers and networks to work at home in lieu of the traditional workplace.
- Employee teams
  - o Work is designed for teams in lieu of individuals.
  - o **Cross-functional teams**
    - Group with mix of specialists that are assigned rather than voluntary membership.
  - o **Project teams**
    - Group specifically to provide a new product or service.
  - o **Self-directed teams**
    - Highly trained workers that are a group that perform interdependent tasks.
  - o **Taskforce teams**
    - Team formed to solve a major organizational issue.
  - o **Process improvement teams**
    - Group assigned with improving quality.
- Flexible work schedules
  - o **Compressed workweek**
    - The number of days in the workweek is shortened and the hours everyday are longer.
  - o **Flextime**
    - Flexible working hours that allow workers options to choose start and end times.
  - o **Job sharing**
    - Two part-time employees share one full time position.

Employee involvement groups (EIs) are groups of employees who meet to resolve problems and improve the organization. There are four steps in EI's:

- Brainstorm ideas for improvement.
- Prepare recommendations for improvement.
- Managers evaluate recommendations and make decisions.
- Recommendations are implemented and the contributors.

86

LIST OF APPENDICES

Appendix	Description
Appendix A	Percentages of Test Topic Questions
Appendix B	Classic Management Perspective
Appendix C	Humanistic Management Perspective
Appendix D	Maslow's Hierarchy of Needs
Appendix E	Types of Departmentalization
Appendix F	Major Federal Employment Laws
Appendix G	Big Five Personality Traits
Appendix H	Emotional Intelligence

APPENDIX A: PERCENTAGES OF TEST TOPIC QUESTIONS

Percentage	Curriculum Content
4%	**Overview of the human resource management field:** • Historical development • Human resource functions • Human resource manager • Motivation, communication, and leadership • Ethical aspects of human resource decision-making
6%	**Human resource planning:** • Strategic human resource issues • Job analysis and job design
15%	**Staffing** • Recruiting • Selection • Promotion and transfers • Reduction-in-force • Voluntary turnover
11%	**Training and development** • Orientation • Career planning • Principles of learning • Training programs and methods • Development programs

Percentage	Curriculum Content
10%	**Performance appraisals** • Reasons for performance evaluation • Techniques • Problems
15%	**Compensation issues** • Job evaluation • Wage and salary administration • Compensation system • Benefits (mandatory and voluntary)
5%	**Safety and health** • Occupational accidents and illness • Quality of work life • Workplace security
5%	**Employee rights and discipline**
15%	**Employment law** • Equal employment opportunity laws • Compensation and benefits laws • Health, safety, and employment laws • Union laws

Percentage	Curriculum Content
6%	**Labor relations** • Unions • Collective bargaining • Unionized versus non-unionized work settings •
4%	**International human resource management**
4%	**Current issues and trends** • Workforce diversity • Human resource information system • Changing patterns of work relationships

APPENDIX B: CLASSIC MANAGEMENT PERSPECTIVE

The classic management perspective emphasizes a rational and scientific approach to management. Below are the major subfields of this study and the characteristics of the approach.

Subfield	Major characteristics
Scientific Management	• To improve labor scientifically proven changes should take place.
Bureaucratic Organizations	• Standard method to job performance. • Select workers with abilities. • Wage incentives for better labor. • Reveal the importance of compensation for performance. • Reveal the importance of the right person for the right job. • Does not focus on social context of jobs. • No individual treatment. • Ignore ideas and suggestions.
Administrative Principles	• Focus on the total organization in lieu of the worker. • **Unity of command** – one person receives orders from one superior. • **Division of work** – work is specialized. • **Unity of direction** – similar activities grouped together. • **Scalar chain** – the chain of command should include every employee.

APPENDIX C: HUMANISTIC MANAGEMENT PERSPECTIVE

The humanistic management perspective focuses on human behavior, needs, and attitudes. Below are the major subfields of this study and the characteristics of the approach.

Subfield	Major characteristics
Human Relations Movement	• Movement that emphasizes satisfaction of basic needs and improves productivity. • Hawthorne studies in 1924 revealed that employees worked better when they had better treatment.
Human Resources Perspective	• Design job to meet higher-level needs (according to Abraham Maslow's hierarchy of needs). • Theory X and Theory Y.
Behavioral Sciences Approach	• Applies social science to organizations.

- The **physiological needs** of life (food, water, shelter, and clothing) are at the base of the triangle.
  - o Basically, if these needs are not reasonably fulfilled, then you cannot ascend to the next step of development.
  - o For example, if you're starving perhaps you aren't focused on safety until the pangs of hunger have been satiated.
- The second building block in the triangle is the need for **safety** and security.
  - o This need includes money, home, and a society that protects against violence.
- The third foundational block includes **social** needs (marriage, friendships, and sexuality).
  - o Satisfying this need resolves feelings of loneliness and isolation.
- After the three foundational needs have been satisfied the next need is for **esteem**.
  - o Esteem includes esteem for self and others. To be respected, and respect others in return. Without

achieving the need for esteem we typically feel worthless and unappreciated.

- The highest point of the triangle is the need for **self-actualization**.
  - o Maslow explains this need as an individual doing what they are "meant" to do.
  - o For instance a writer should write, a singer should sing, and an actor should act.
  - o When going through the self-actualization phase we feel a sense of restlessness as we struggle to achieve our destiny.
  - o Self-actualization is the discovering of your place in the universe.

Maslow referred to those that did reach self-actualization as **Transcenders** and **Theory Z** people. He also opined that they were the happiest, most well adjusted people of all. Striving to be all that you are meant to can increase your satisfaction with your life.

Vertical Functional

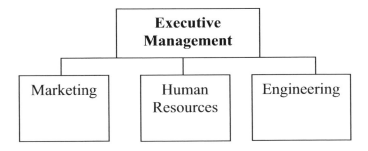

Divisional

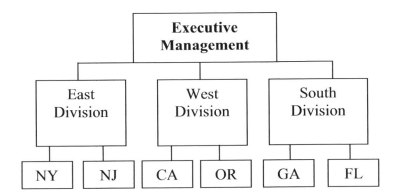

Year	Law	Effect
1963	Equal Pay Act	No difference in pay based on gender.
1964	Civil Rights Act, Title VII	No discrimination based on gender, age, color, religion, national origin.
1967	Age Discrimination in Employment	Restricts mandatory retirement and outlaws age discrimination.
1970	Occupational Safety and Health Act (OSHA)	Mandatory safety standards in the workplace.
1972	Equal Employment Opportunity Act	Coverage of the Civil Rights Act of 1964 broadened to state and local governments and public and private educational institutions.
1978	Pregnancy Discrimination Act of 1978	Cannot discriminate against a woman because of pregnancy.
1990	Americans with Disabilities Act	Prevents discrimination against employees who are physically or mentally handicap.
1991	Civil Rights Act	No discrimination based on sex, religion, national origin, and disability. The discriminated against can seek damages from the employer.
1993	Family Medical Leave Act (FMLA)	Employers to provide up to 12 weeks of unpaid leave after childbirth, adoption, or familial emergency.
1994	Uniformed Services Employment and Reemployment Rights	People who go to the military for a short service have their home jobs secure in their absence.

APPENDIX G: BIG FIVE PERSONALITY TRAITS

Trait	Definition
Extroversion	Degree of talkativeness, assertiveness, and comfort with relationships.
Agreeableness	Degree of cooperation, forgiveness, understanding, and trust.
Conscientiousness	Degree of responsibility, dependability, and achievement orientation.
Emotional stability	Degree of serenity, enthusiasm, and security.
Openness to experience	Degree of interests, imagination, creativity, and consideration of novel ideas.

Appendix H: Emotional Intelligence

Trait	Definition
Self-awareness	Ability to be aware of self-feeling.
Managing emotions	Ability to control moods.
Motivating oneself	Ability to face obstacles and pursue goals.
Empathy	Ability to recognize what others are feeling.
Social skill	Ability to connect with others in a positive way.

GLOSSARY

Because this is a study guide, some of these words are found throughout the text, however there are some new ones, be sure you understand the meanings to all of these words because they will help you exponentially during the multiple choice test. Remember what you can, make flashcards for the rest, and quiz yourself a lot, you won't regret it!

360-degree feedback – process that uses multiple raters to appraise employees and guide in development

A

Absenteeism - not reporting to work

Accountability – the idea that people with authority are subject to reporting to superiors

Achievement tests – tests that measure what a person can do right now

Active listening- listening to understand without judgment

Adverse impact – rejection of higher percentage of a protected class for employment when compared with non protected class

Affirmative action – policy that requires employers to guarantee equal employment for people in minority groups

Alarm reaction – response to stress characterized by elevated heart rate, increased respiration, and adrenaline

Alternative dispute resolution - different types of employee complaint resolution procedures

Aptitude tests – measures what a person is capable of learning

Arbitrator – neutral third-party who resolves disputes

Assessment center – process where individuals are evaluated to see if they have the skills needed for a job

Augmented skills – skills helpful for expatriate (out of country) managers

Authority – the right to tell people what to do

Authorization card – statement signed by employee empowering union to negotiate on their behalf

Autocratic leader – leader who centralizes authority and relies on legitimate, reward, and coercive power to manage subordinates

Autonomy – degree to which a job gives freedom, independence, scheduling, and procedures

B

Balance-sheet approach– compensation system designed to match purchasing power in a country

Bargaining power – power union has to collectively negotiate for many people

Bargaining unit – group of two or more employees who can be grouped together for bargaining

Bargaining zone – area where union and organization will concede during bargaining

Behavioral modeling – behavioral approach that demonstrates a desired behavior and gives the trainees a chance to practice through role-play

Behavior modification – changing behavior based on reinforcement

Behavioral observation scale (BOS) – measures frequency of observed behavior

Behavioral description interview (BDI) – asks questions about what she or he did in a situation

Behaviorally anchored rating scale (BARS) – rating technique that judges an employee's performance on job

Benchmarking – process of measuring products, services, and practices against competitors

Big five model –five factor personality model that includes: extraversion, agreeableness, conscientiousness, emotional stability, and openness to experience

Bona fide occupational qualification (BFOQ) – suitable defense against discrimination where race, age, religion, sex, or nationality is a qualification for the job

Bonus – incentive payment

Bounded rationality – people only have time to process a certain amount of information

Burnout – most severe stage of distress characterized by lack or productivity, depression, and frustration

Business unionism – term for goals of labor organizations (wages, hours, job security, and working conditions)

C

Career counseling – discussing with employees their current job activities, personal interests and goals and career objectives

Career paths – line of advancement

Career plateau – probability of career advancement low

Chain of command – unbroken line of authority

Charge form – discrimination complaint filed with EEOC

Codetermination – representation of labor on board of directors of an organization

Collective bargaining process – negotiating agreements with the use of economic pressure

Combined salary and commission plan – compensation that includes salary and commission

Comparable worth – concept that jobs that are not similar but equal in terms of value should be paid the same (despite gender)

Compensation – monetary and non-monetary rewards for work

Compensatory model – selection decision where a high score in one area can compensate a low score in another

Competence based pay – pay based on employee's skill and knowledge level

Competency assessment – analysis of the skills needed for knowledge intensive jobs

Compressed woweek- employees stay longer per day, but have shorter weeks

Computer assisted instruction (CAI) – interactive format for instruction

Computer managed instruction (CMI) – usually employed with CAI using a computer to generate and score tests and assess proficiency

Concurrent validity – extent which test scores match the data obtained at same time from employees

Conflict – disagreement

Construct validity – extent which selection teal measures a trait

Constructive discharge – employee resigns because of unreasonable employment conditions

Consumer price index (CPI) – measurement of average change in prices over time in the market place

Content validity – extent which selection instrument adequately assesses knowledge and skills

Continuous reinforcement schedule – every desired behavior is reinforced

Contrast error – performance-rating error on an evaluation because the person is being compared to the previous evaluation

Contributory plan – pension plan where both organization and employee make contributions

Cooperative training – combination of on the job training with formal education classes

Core competence- organization's specialty that they do better than their competitors

Core skills – skills that are crucial to an employee abroad

Craft unions – unions that represent skilled craft workers

Criterion related validity – extent which selection tool predicts important work behavior elements

Critical incident – event that denotes superior or inferior employee performance

Critical incident method – important job tasks are identified for job success

Cross training – training employees in jobs related to their own (job rotation)

Cross validation – verifying results of one test with the results from a different test

Cultural audits – audits of culture and quality of work life in the organization

Cultural environment - people and their values and beliefs

Culture shock – feeling of confusion and disorientation when submersed in a different culture

Cumulative trauma disorders – injuries of hand, finger, and wrist caused by repetitive motions

Customer appraisal – performance appraisal based on TQM seeking evaluation from internal and external environment

D

Data – unanalyzed facts and figures

Decruitment- techniques for reducing labor supply within the organization (layoffs, firings, transfers, and job sharing)

Defense mechanism – emotional blocks to protect self

Defined benefit plan – pension plan where amount is identified that employee will receive at retirement

Defined contribution plan – pension plan that establishes the basis, which an employer will contribute to the pension

Depression – negative emotion associated with gloom, sadness, and loss of interest in normal activities

Differential piece rate – compensation structure where when employee production exceeds standard output they receive a higher rate for all work than those that do not exceed

Disabled individual – person who has physical mental impairment, record of the impairment, and is regarded as having the impairment

Discipline – punishment or orderly behavior in an organization or training that molds and strengthens

Discrimination – hiring or promoting based on criteria that is not relevant to the job

Disparate treatment – when protected class has a different evaluation system than a non-protected class

Distress – harmful stress characterized by feelings of inadequacy

Downsizing – planned elimination of jobs

Dual career partnerships – couples that follow their own careers and support each other

Due process – employee's right to present their position during discipline

E

Earnings at risk incentives – incentive pay that puts a part of the employee's pay at risk, but gives them a chance to earn extra pay

EEO-1 report – annual form that has to be filed annually for anyone employing over 100 people to determine a company's workforce composition

Effectiveness- the degree which an organization achieves its goals

Efficiency – degree which an organization achieves its goals with less resources

Ego strength – degree of strength in a person's convictions

Elder care – care provided to an employee's elderly family members

Employee assistance programs (EAP) – programs that help employees work through personal problems that interfere with job performance

Employee associations – labor organizational that represent professional employees in labor management

Employee involvement groups – group of employees that meet in an attempt to resolve problems

Employee leasing – dismissing employees who are hired on by a leasing company to handle the HR functions while the employee is leased back to the organization

Employee rights – fair treatment (especially privacy)

Employee stock ownership plans (ESOPs) – organization contributes shares of stock to a trust for purchase by employees

Employee teams – work functions are divided into groups (in lieu of individuals) and team is given self-management

Employment at will principle – the right of an employer to fire an employee without a reason

Empowerment – delegation of power to subordinates

Entrepreneur – one who starts, organizers, manages, and assumes responsibility for an organization

Equal employment opportunity (EEO) – treatment of individuals is fair

Equity theory – theory that examines people's perceptions of equality

ERG theory – simplified hierarchy theory with three stages: existence, relatedness, and growth

Ergonomics – specifically designed equipment that can be used efficiently and with promotes comfort

Error of central tendency – performance-rating problem where all employees are rated about average

Essay method – approach to performance appraisal that requires the evaluator to compose a statement that describes the behavior being rated

Ethical dilemma – situation where all choices are undesirable

Ethics – moral values

Ethnocentrism – belief that one culture group is better than another

Ethnorelativism – belief that culture groups are equal

Eustress – good stress that motivates someone to do better

Exclusive representation – legal right of union to represent all bargaining members equally whether they have joined the union or not

Exempt employees – employees not covered under the Fair Labor Standards Act (FLSA)

Exit interview – interview with leaving employees to find out why they are leaving

Expatriates – employees who live and work in a different country than their own

Expectancy theory – motivations depend on people's expectations of rewards

External fit – work system supports the organization's goals

Extrinsic reward – reward given by another

F

Factor comparison system – evaluation accomplished on factor-by-factor basis

Failure rate – percentage of expatriates who are unsatisfactory

Fair employment practices – state and local laws that govern equal employment opportunity (usually more specific than the federal laws)

Fair representation doctrine – unions' legal obligation to provide assistance to member and nonmembers in labor relations

Fast-track program – program encouraging young managers with high potential to remain in an organization with quick promotions

Flexible benefits plans (cafeteria plans) – enable individuals to choose the benefits that suit their needs the best

Flextime – scheduling freedom for employees as long as they put the same amount of hours in

Forced-choice method – performance appraisal method that requires rater to choose from statements that distinguishes between satisfactory and unsatisfactory performance

Formal communication channel – communication that is defined by chain of command

Four-fifths rule – rule of thumb followed by EEOC to determine adverse impact of enforcement

Frustration – regression principle – idea that if one need cannot be met the individual will regress to a lower, already met need

Functional job analysis – quantitative job analysis that evaluates data, people, and things

Fundamental attribution error – underestimate external factors on behavior

G

Gainsharing plans – programs that share the financial gains based on a formula that reflects productivity

General adaptation syndrome (GAS) – physiological response to stimuli that begins with alertness, goes to response, and ends in exhaustion if the response is long enough

Glass ceiling – invisible barriers in business for minorities and women

Global outsourcing – using foreign labor to save money

Grapevine – informal communication channel (gossip)

Graphic rating scale method – performance appraisal where each employee is rated based on characteristics

Grievance procedure – formal procedure that provides for union to address grievances for members and nonmembers

Guest workers – foreign workers invited to perform needed labor

H

Halo effect – assuming someone is good at everything because they are good at one thing

Hawthorne studies – studies conducted in 1924 that revealed that people work better when treatment improves

Hay profile method – job evaluation that uses knowledge, mental activity, and accountability to evaluate

Health Maintenance Organization (HMO) – organizations of doctors and health care professionals that provide services based on prepaid basis

Heuristics – rules of thumb

Hierarchy of needs theory – developed by Abraham Maslow with five categories (physiological, safety, belonging, esteem, and self-actualization)

High performance work system (HPWS) – specific combination of HR practices that are used to maximize employee knowledge, skills, and flexibility

Horizontal communication – communication among peers

Host country – country where an international company operates

Host-country nationals – people who are natives to the host country and work in the organization

Hot stove rule – discipline – warning, effective, enforced consistently, and applies to all employees fairly

Human capital – employees' skills, capabilities, and experience

Human relations movement – movement that highlighted the treatment of the employees

Human resource information system (HRIS) – HR system that provides accurate data to aid with decisions

Human resource management – activities to attract, develop, and retain a good staff

Human resources perspective – perspective that believes that jobs should be tailored to meet the higher level needs of the employee and help them reach their full potential

Humanistic perspective – management perspective emphasizing the workers needs

Human resources planning – process of planning for people to move in, within, and out of organization

Hygiene factors – factors that influence job satisfaction (work conditions, company policies, pay)

I

Idea incubator – in-house safe-house for ideas for change in an organization

Implementation – putting a plan into action

Improshare – gainsharing program where bonuses are based on overall productivity

In basket training – assessment center with simulation of real life work situation

Individualism – expectation that people take care of themselves

Individualism approach – if the act will be the best in the long-run for the individual, then it is moral

Industrial engineering – field of study analyzing work methods

Industrial union – unions that represent people across industries

Information – data converted to meaning

Infrastructure – country's ability to support economics (roads, etc)

Internal environment – atmosphere inside the organization

Instructional objectives – goals of training

Interest based bargaining – problem solving with a win/win philosophy

Internal fit – internal elements complement one another

International corporation – domestic organization that moves into foreign countries

International dimension – external environment that represents events in foreign environments that impact the organization

Internship program – programs sponsored by colleges, universities, and organizations that offer students real life work experience in exchange for networking and resume experience

Intrinsic reward – pleasurable feeling someone gets from conducting an activity (motivated from the inside)

Intuition – unconscious apprehension

J

Job – group of duties

Job analysis – determining duties, tasks, and responsibilities of a job

Job characteristics model – job design that supports meaningfulness, responsibility, and knowledge

113

Job classification system – jobs grouped into a series of wage grades

Job description – statement of tasks, expectations, and duties related to the job

Job design – improves jobs through technological or human considerations to improve productivity and satisfaction

Job enlargement- making a job more challenging

Job enrichment – making a job more meaningful

Job evaluation – determining the value of a job

Job family – group of individual but similar jobs

Job posting and bidding – posting vacancies and maintaining lists of employees looking for promotions

Job progression – hierarchy of jobs from new person to successful manager

Job ranking system – jobs are arranged by worth

Job rotation – moves employees to different jobs for variety

Job satisfaction – positive attitude toward a job

Job simplification – making a job less challenging

Job specification – statement of needed skills, knowledge and abilities for the position

Justice approach – moral decisions are fair and impartial

K

Knowledge management – effort to organize and make available the corporate knowledge within an organization

Knowledge workers – workers whose job extends beyond physical position to plan, decision-making, and problem solving

L

Labor market – the prospective employees of an organization

Labor relations process – four events: workers want collective bargaining, unions organize, collective negotiations lead to a contract, contract is signed

Labor union – organization seeking to protect its individuals through collective bargaining

Law of effect – positive reinforced behavior is repeated and unreinforced or negatively reinforced behavior is not repeated

Leaderless group discussions – assessment center process where training are in a conference to discuss a topic with or without assigned roles

Leadership – ability to influence

Learning organization – everyone is engaged in solving problems and attempts to improve the organization

Leniency or strictness error – performance-rating error where appraiser gives employees either really high or really low marks

Locus of control – where the person places the responsibility of success of failure (internal – in oneself, or external – outside factors)

Lump-sum merit program – employees receive a year-end payment that is not added to their base salary

M

Machiavellianism – manipulating others for power and personal gain

Management – attaining organizational goals by planning, leading, and controlling the organization

Management by objectives (MBO) – rates performance on employee achievement of goals that were set by mutual agreement

Management by wandering around (MBWA) – communication where managers interact with workers

Management forecasts – opinions of management for organization's future needs

Manager appraisal – performance appraisal performed by a supervisor or manager, which is reviewed by one level higher

Managing diversity – being aware of characteristic differences of employees and managing people as individuals

Markov analysis – tracking employment movement through jobs

Masculinity – focus on achievement and assertiveness

Mediation – third party resolution to conflict

Mediator – third party person that meets one conflicting group, then the other to reach a compromise

Medical savings account (MSA) – medical insurance financed by employer contributions to an employee's medical savings

Mentor – more experience person that teaches less experienced person

Merit guidelines – rules for awards tied to performance objectives

Mission – reason for an organization to exist

Mission statement – statement that defines the reason for the organization's existence

Mixed standards scale method – trait performance appraisal with adjectives: better than, equal to, or worse than

Monoculture – culture that accepts only one set of values and beliefs

Moral-rights approach – moral decisions are ones that retain the individual's moral rights

Motivation – direction to accomplish something

Motivators – factors that influence motivation

Multinational Corporation – received more than 25 percent of its sales outside the home country

Multiple cutoff model – requires applicant to achieve minimum proficiency in all dimensions

Multiple hurdle model – only applicants with highest scores on initial tests move to next

N

Negligence – failure to give care with the result of injury

Nepotism – hiring of relatives over current employees

Noncontributory plan – pension plan where the employer makes all contributions

Nondirective interview – interview where applicant is given freedom in leading the discussion

Nonexempt employees – employees covered under the Fair Labor Standards Act

Nonprogrammed decision – responsive decision based on situation

Nonverbal communication – communications transmitted in a form other than words

Norm – standard of conduct

O

Ombudsman – individual designated to receive complains and resolution from employees

Omnipotent view of management – idea that managers are responsible for success of failure of an organization (opposite of symbolic view)

On the job training (OJT) – training that is conducted as the employee is learning from a more experienced person on the job

Open door policy – settling grievances through various levels of management (not necessary to follow the exact chain of command)

Organization – structured entity with a goal

Organization analysis – examination of environment, strategies, and resources of an organization

Organization capability – organization's ability to adapt and change to keep an advantage over the competition

Organization chart – visual depiction of the organizational structure

Organizational behavior – a behavioral science that explores individuals and groups in organizations

Organizational citizenship – work behavior that is beyond the job requirements that contribute to the success of an organization

Organizational commitment – loyalty to an organization

Organizational control – process which mangers regulate the activities to make them consistent with goals

Organizational development (OD) – behavioral science that targets improving effectiveness of organization

Orientation – introduction to an organization and the rules and regulations it has

Outplacement services – services that help organization's terminated employees find a new job

Outsourcing – finding outside people to perform jobs that were done inside the organization

P

Panel interview – an interview with two or more people asking questions to a single applicant

Parochialism – inability to recognize differences in people

Partial reinforcement schedule – some occurrences are rewarded and some are not

Path goal theory – contingency approach where leadership is responsible for clarifying rewards and consequences

Pay equity – employee's perception that pay is in equal value to work

Pay for performance – compensation based on job performance and effort

Peer appraisal – appraisal done by fellow employees usually compiled and delivered to employee by a manager

Peer review system – reviewing method of grievances by voting on resolutions

Perception – how people sense the environment

Perceptual defense – protection by disregarding threatening concepts

Perceptual distortion – inaccuracies in perception

Perceptual selectivity – how people select what to pay attention to

Performance appraisal – feedback on performance

Performance gap – difference between performance expectation and actual performance

Personality – characteristics that dictate behavior

Perquisites – sometimes referred to as perks they are the special benefits given to executives

Person analysis – determination of who needs training

Piecework – work paid by the number produced

Point system – determination of the value of a job by the points assigned

Political forces – culture in an organization that guides the power structure among people

Position – job of one employee

Positive discipline – focuses on early correction of misconduct with the employee correcting the problem

Power – ability to influence

Power distance – degree of inequality acceptance from individuals in the organization

Proactive change – change targeted to specific opportunities

Process audit – determination of if a high performance work system is implemented

Profit sharing – employer pays deferred sums based on the profits of the company

Programmed decision – choice made about a situation that has recurred often enough for the decision-maker to rely on past choices

Projection – set personal traits on others

Promotion – change to a higher level in an organization

Protected classes – minority people that are covered under the Equal Employment Opportunity laws

Q

Quality circle – group of 6-12 that meet regularly to discuss organizational issues

Quality of life – emphasizes relationship to others

Quantity of life – emphasizes assertiveness, money, and material goods

R

Reactive change – change when outside factors have already influenced performance

Real wages – wage increases larger than the consumer price index

Realistic job preview (RJP) – informing applicants about the job (even undesirable portions of it)

Reasonable accommodation – reasonable changes made for disabled people or people of a different religion to perform a job

Recency error – error in appraisal to base all of factors on employee's most recent behavior

Recordable case – any case to be recorded in OSHA form 300

Red circle rates – payment rates above the pay range

Recruiting – attempt to find quality staff

Reengineering – radical redesign

Reliability – degree which interviews and tests give a predictable result of job performance

Relocation services – organization transfers employee to a new location

Repatriation – employee transfers home from an international assignment

Replacement charts – listing of people in jobs and replacement people in cases of vacancies

Resources – assets of an organization (human, financial, cultural, intangible, and physical)

Responsibility – duty to perform a task that is assigned

Responsibility center – organizational unit under one person

Reverse discrimination – giving preferences to protected classes to extent that unprotected classes are being discriminated against

Right to know laws – laws that require employer to advise about hazmat materials they are handling

Rights arbitration – arbitration over meaning of contract terms or grievances

Risk propensity – individual's willingness to accept risk

Role – set of expectations of behavior

Role ambiguity – cause for work stress when the person does not know what is expected of them

Role conflict – incompatible roles in the organization

Rucker plan – bonuses based on earnings of hourly employees and their production value

Satisficing – implementing first acceptable decision even if it may not be the best one

Scanlon plan – bonus for gaining cost reduction

Selection ratio – number of applicants and number of positions

Self-appraisal – performance appraisal that is completed on self-performance prior to formal appraisal

Self-serving bias – overestimate internal factors to success

Sexual harassment – unwelcome advances, requests, and verbal or physical sexual contact

Silver handshake – early retirement incentive with a bonus or increased retirement benefits

Similar to me error – appraisal error where the appraiser inflates the evaluation because they are personable

Situational interview – interviewee given a hypothetical situation

Six Sigma – process used to translate customer needs with a low cost way to provide them

Skill inventories – files of experience, interest, education, skills, and abilities for employees so management can quickly match people with openings

Social forces – culture in an organization that guides the relationships with the people

Span of management – number of employees per supervisor

Spot bonus – unplanned bonus given to an employee for their effort

Staffing tables – graph representing jobs, and the number of employees

Standard hour plan – incentive plan that rewards for completion in a specific time

Step review system – reviewing employee grievances by successively going to higher levels of management

Stereotyping- making judgments on someone based on a few characteristics

Straight commission plan – compensation based on a percentage of the sale

Straight piecework – pay per unit produced

Straight salary plan – compensation for sales people for doing other duties not related to a sale

Stress – physiological or emotional response that places demands on a person

Structured interview – standardized questions having a set of answers is used

Subordinate appraisal – appraisal of a supervisor by an employee (usually used for development purposes)

Succession planning – identifying people for successive positions

Supplemental unemployment benefits – plan through an employer where the laid off employee can draw off of a fund created for the laid off workers

Symbolic view of management- idea that outside factors are mostly responsible for the success or failure of an organization (opposite of omnipotent view)

Synergy – condition where the whole is greater than the sum of the parts

T

Task analysis – determination of content of a training program based on the tasks of a job

Team appraisal – performance appraisal based on team not individual efforts

Team incentive plan – incentive pay for team when they have met or exceeded standards

Telecommuting – working from remote location through technology

Theory X- people are basically lazy and must be coerced to work

Theory Y- people like to work and can exercise self-direction

Third country nationals – employees who are from a country that is not the host or home country

Total quality management – focuses on total organization by involvement, customer focus, benchmarking, and improvement

Transfer – moving an employee laterally in the organization

Transfer of training – effectively using the skills learned in training on the job

Transnational corporation – balances local responsiveness to a global scale

Turnover – the amount of voluntary and involuntary withdrawal from an organization

Type A personality – extreme competitiveness, impatience, aggression, and work devotion

Type B personality – balanced, relaxed, and laid back lifestyle

U

Unfair labor practices (ULPs) – practices by a union or employer that deny a person their rights under the federal labor laws

Uniform Guidelines on Employee Selection Procedures – procedures published by the government to assist organizational in complying with regulations

Union shop – labor agreement that spells out that people must be in the union in order to gain employment

Union steward – nonpaid union official representing members with management

Utilitarian approach – the greatest good to the greatest amount of people is a moral decision

V

Validity – degree that something correctly measures what it is meant to

Validity generalization – validity of coefficients that can be generalized across multiple situations

Value added compensation – evaluation of compensation program for advancing the needs of the employees and goals of the organization

Variable pay – pay is linked to performance

Vesting – guarantee of benefits at retirement age regardless of employment

Virtual team – team linked via electronic means

Voluntary protection programs (VPPs) – programs that encourage organizations to surpass OSHA standards

Vision – ideal future of an organization

W

Wage and salary survey – survey of wages paid to employees by other employers in the same labor market

Wage curve – graphical representation of the relationship between worth of job and wage

Wage rate compensation – differential between job classes (hourly workers and managers)

Work permit – government document authorizing employment of foreign individual

Workers' compensation insurance – insurance used to help cover the loss of income when someone is hurt on the job

Workforce utilization analysis – classifying protected-class workers by the number and types of jobs in an organization

If you can answer about half of the questions correctly you should be in good shape. To be safe, strive for a 75% on this examination.

1. Which of the following is an example of an intrinsic reward?
    a. Doing a job because the employee likes it
    b. Doing a job because the boss will give a bonus
    c. Doing a job for a positive appraisal performance
    d. Doing a job for a reward

2. Which of the following schools of thought to motivation focuses on economic rewards to motivate performance?
    a. Traditional
    b. Human relations
    c. Human resources
    d. Contemporary

3. Which definition is correct for outsourcing?
    a. Using another country's labor resources.
    b. Tapping another country's demands.
    c. Managing a production facility abroad.
    d. Form of licensing that provides foreign entity with guidance.

4. Which of the following performance appraisal methods are the most expensive to develop, keep relevant, and are susceptible to errors?
    a. Trait
    b. Behavioral
    c. Results
    d. Balanced score card

Use the following for questions 5-8.

    I. Subordinate appraisal
    II. Peer appraisal
    III. Manager/supervisor appraisal
    IV. 360 degree appraisal

5. The combination of various appraisals that give the employee and manager the best view at the employee's performance.
    a. I
    b. II
    c. III
    d. IV

6. Not an advisable appraisal method when peers are competing for positions or bonuses.
    a. I
    b. II
    c. III
    d. IV

7. The most traditional (but likely not most effective) appraisal method.
    a. I
    b. II
    c. III
    d. IV

8. An appraisal that is typically used for developmental purposes only.
    a. I
    b. II
    c. III
    d. IV

9. Which of the following is not true of a learning organization?
    a. Participatory in problem solving
    b. Celebrates risks
    c. Values individuality
    d. Empowers employees with freedom of resources

10. A rating method that requires the rater to choose from statements that best describe the employee's performance.
      a. Graphic rating scale
      b. Mixed standard scale
      c. Force-choice
      d. Essay

11. The _____ is when someone is rated the same based on just a few attributes.
      a. Contrast error
      b. Similar to me error
      c. Halo effect
      d. Error of central tendency

12. What job evaluation system does the federal government use?
      a. Job ranking
      b. Job classification
      c. Point system
      d. Factor comparison system

13. Which of the following would the employee assistance program not cover?
      a. Marriage counseling
      b. Cancer treatments
      c. Financial assistance for childcare
      d. Dependent care spending account

14. The law that specifies after a year with an employer with health insurance a worker can transfer insurance to another employer.
      a. COBRA
      b. HMO
      c. HIPAA
      d. EAP

15. Which of the following is the removal of something unpleasant when a desired behavior is exhibited?
      a. Positive reinforcement
      b. Negative reinforcement
      c. Punishment
      d. Extinction

16. What is eustress?
    a. A type of stress that impacts the heart
    b. A good stress that strives people to accomplish
    c. A bad stress that is harmful
    d. The stress right before burnout (extreme stress)

Use the following for questions 17-20
    I.   Vesting
    II.   Non-contributory
    III.   Defined-benefit
    IV.   401(k)

17. Only the employer funds the pensions (no deduction from the employee's salary).
    a. I
    b. II
    c. III
    d. IV

18. Period of time until the guarantee of benefits
    a. I
    b. II
    c. III
    d. IV

19. Today's main source of retirement funds with a typical employer match.
    a. I
    b. II
    c. III
    d. IV

20. In the _____ the amount an employee will receive is specific and not based on stock-market conditions.
    a. I
    b. II
    c. III
    d. IV

21. Examines how people will strive for perceived fairness by changing inputs, outcomes, distort perception, or leave the job.
    a. ERG
    b. Maslow's Hierarchy of Needs
    c. Hygiene/Motivators
    d. Equity

22. Which of the following contemporary approaches to motivation believes that few people reach the top level of motivation, and those that do are called "transcenders"?
    a. McClelland's Acquired Needs Theory
    b. Herzberg's Two-Factor Theory
    c. McGregor's Theory X and Theory Y
    d. Maslow's Hierarchy of Needs Theory

23. Approach to discipline that it is effective, consistent, and applied equally.
    a. Fairness doctrine
    b. Hot-stove approach
    c. Positive reinforcement
    d. Punishment

24. Which of the following is true of a learning organization?
    a. Autocratic in problem solving.
    b. Celebrates stability and reliability.
    c. Focuses on individual versus teamwork.
    d. Empowers employees to take risks.

Use the following for questions 25-28
    I.   Open-door policy
    II.   Ombudsman system
    III.   Mediation
    IV.   Step-review system

25. Alternative resolution procedure that employs a neutral party to hear both sides and renders a compromise.
    a. I
    b. II
    c. III
    d. IV

26. Dispute settlement with various levels of management.
   a. I
   b. II
   c. III
   d. IV

27. Designated employee that others can seek out for counsel.
   a. I
   b. II
   c. III
   d. IV

28. Resolution via successive higher levels of management.
   a. I
   b. II
   c. III
   d. IV

29. How many years does HR have to keep a copy of the I-9?
   a. 1
   b. 3
   c. 4
   d. 6

Use the following for questions 30-33
   I.   McDonnell Douglas test
   II.   Adverse impact
   III.   Disparate treatment
   IV.   Four-fifths rule

30. Unintentional discrimination is _____.
   a. I
   b. II
   c. III
   d. IV

31. Intentional discrimination is _____.
   a. I
   b. II
   c. III
   d. IV

32. The calculation in figuring out discrimination hearings.
        a. I
        b. II
        c. III
        d. IV

33. If _____ is met, a person can file a suit against an organization.
        a. I
        b. II
        c. III
        d. IV

34. _____ is when an individual stops advancing in an organization before reaching the highest rung of the organization.
        a. Career plateauing
        b. Exhaustive career path
        c. Fast-tracking
        d. Discriminatory practices

35. Under OSHA law the _____ level is the inspection based on employee complaints of violations.
        a. First
        b. Second
        c. Third
        d. Fourth

Use the following for questions 36-39.
        I. Taft-Harley Act
        II. Landrum-Griffin Act
        III. Wagner Act
        IV. Fair Labor Standards Act

36. Act that determined "exempt" and "non-exempt" employees.
        a. I
        b. II
        c. III
        d. IV

37. Act that allowed state labor relations to rule on cases that the National Labor Relations Board would not consider.
    a. I
    b. II
    c. III
    d. IV

38. Pro-business act that banned union closed-shop practices.
    a. I
    b. II
    c. III
    d. IV

39. Act that guarantees the right to form a union.
    a. I
    b. II
    c. III
    d. IV

40. Which of the following may not be included in a background check?
    a. Criminal convictions check
    b. Previous employers
    c. Credit
    d. Religious affiliation

Use the following for questions 41-44
    I.   ERG Theory
    II.   Theory X and Theory Y
    III. Two-Factor Theory
    IV.   Acquired Needs Theory

41. A modification of Maslow's Hierarchy of Needs that focuses on three motivating factors.
    a. I
    b. II
    c. III
    d. IV

42. Theory that focuses on hygiene and motivator needs.
    a. I
    b. II
    c. III
    d. IV

43. Theory created by Douglas McGregor.
    a. I
    b. II
    c. III
    d. IV

44. Theory that focuses on achievement, affiliation, and power.
    a. I
    b. II
    c. III
    d. IV

45. Ethical decision based on the greatest good for the greatest amount of people is:
    a. Moral-rights
    b. Utilitarian
    c. Justice
    d. Integrative social theory

46. What does BFOQ stand for?
    a. Bona Fide Occupational Qualification
    b. Business Fidelity Occupational Qualification
    c. Business Fitness Occupational Quality
    d. Bona Fide Occupational Quality

47. Which of the following specifies a minimum wage for workers under federal contracts for construction?
    a. Equal Pay Act
    b. Walsh-Healy Act
    c. Davis-Bacon Act
    d. Fair Labor Standards Act

48. A company with at least ___ number of employees is subject to the Family Medical Leave Act.
    a. 10
    b. 25
    c. 40
    d. 50

49. Which of the following is not a focus of the Hackman/Oldman Characteristics model?
    a. Core job dimensions
    b. Critical psychological states
    c. Employee growth need
    d. All of the above

50. Which of the following job characteristics identify the degree which employee performs a job from beginning to ending?
    a. Autonomy
    b. Skill variety
    c. Task identity
    d. Task significance

51. Which of the following is a question you CAN ask at an interview?
    a. Are you married?
    b. Are you a United States citizen?
    c. What year did you graduate high school?
    d. Have you ever been arrested?

52. What is the term applied to the unions responsibility to represent union and non-union members equally?
    a. Fair doctrine
    b. Equity doctrine
    c. Fair representation
    d. Equal representation

53. The process of an employee returning from a host country is called _____.
    a. Reintegration
    b. Repatriation
    c. Re-immigration
    d. None of the above

54. What type of reinforcement schedule are paydays associated with?
    a. Fixed-interval
    b. Fixed ratio
    c. Variable interval
    d. Variable ratio

Use the following for questions 55-58
    I.   Job simplification
    II.   Job enlargement
    III.   Job rotation
    IV.   Job enrichment

55. _____ is when management moves employees to different jobs to give variety.
    a. I
    b. II
    c. III
    d. IV

56. _____ is the use of motivators (responsibility, recognition, growth) to increase job satisfaction.
    a. I
    b. II
    c. III
    d. IV

57. _____ is the improvement of efficiency of a job which is typically met with resistance by the workers.
    a. I
    b. II
    c. III
    d. IV

58. _____ is the process of making a job more complex.
    a. I
    b. II
    c. III
    d. IV

59. How many weeks does unemployment insurance cover?
    a. 12
    b. 52
    c. 26
    d. 6

60. Which act states that any business with over 100 employees that has a mass layoff plan must supply advanced notice?
   a. WARN
   b. OSHA
   c. SAF-T
   d. Wagner

Use the following for questions 61-64
   I.   Legitimate
   II.   Reward
   III. Coercive
   IV.   Expert

61. The power that is based on a person's specialized skill and knowledge.
   a. I
   b. II
   c. III
   d. IV

62. The power that is based on the organizational structure and the manager's authority to punish.
   a. I
   b. II
   c. III
   d. IV

63. The power that is built in to the structure of the organization based on position.
   a. I
   b. II
   c. III
   d. IV

64. The power that is based on the organizational structure and the manager's authority to give incentives.
   a. I
   b. II
   c. III
   d. IV

65. What are the three types of interviews?
   a. Structured, unstructured, panel
   b. Simulation, stress, panel
   c. Panel, stress, unstructured
   d. Structured, unstructured, stress

66. What is the silver handshake?
   a. A bonus presented in front of peers to reward good behavior.
   b. A promise for fast tracking upon hiring.
   c. The promise to keep trade secrets even after employment.
   d. Early retirement incentives to avoid layoffs.

67. _____ is when the employer makes work-life so difficult that the employee has no choice but resignation.
   a. Termination
   b. Firing
   c. Constructive discharge
   d. Discrimination

68. The Age Discrimination and Employment Act covers people of what ages?
   a. All ages
   b. Under 30
   c. Over 40
   d. Over Social Security retirement age

Use the following for questions 69-72
   I.   Punishment
   II.   Negative reinforcement
   III. Positive reinforcement
   IV.   Extinction

69. A monetary bonus for excellent sales is an example of:
   a. I
   b. II
   c. III
   d. IV

70. The withdrawal of a reward.
    a. I
    b. II
    c. III
    d. IV

71. The removal of unpleasant stimuli with a desired behavior.
    a. I
    b. II
    c. III
    d. IV

72. Unpleasant stimuli for an undesired behavior.
    a. I
    b. II
    c. III
    d. IV

73. A method of evaluating management positions based on knowledge, mental activity, and accountability.
    a. Hay profile
    b. Factor comparison
    c. Point
    d. Job ranking

74. Payment based on the number of units produced.
    a. Salary
    b. Piecework
    c. Hourly
    d. Overtime

75. The law that specifies that employers must make health coverage available at the same rate the employers would pay in the event of termination of employment, divorce, or death.
    a. COBRA
    b. WARN
    c. OWBPA
    d. Social Security Act

76. What does Executive Order 11246 cover?
    a. Reemployment of returning military
    b. Control over hiring illegal immigrants
    c. Mandate to fill out the EEO-1 report annually
    d. Federal agencies and government contractors must comply with anti-discrimination laws

77. According to Abraham Maslow's Hierarchy of Needs what need is at the top of the pyramid?
    a. Physiological
    b. Security
    c. Belonging
    d. Self Actualization

78. Which of the following is not a definition of a disability?
    a. Mental or physical impairment that limits activities
    b. Impairment recorded
    c. Person is regarded as having impairment
    d. They all are a definition of a disability

79. What are the five personality factors in the Big Five model?
    a. Extraversion, agreeableness, conscientiousness, emotional stability, openness to experience.
    b. Extraversion, conflict avoidance, ability to empathize, charitable ideas, and adventuresome.
    c. Ability to project emotions, conflict avoidance, openness to experience, emotional stability, intelligence.
    d. Intelligence, creativity, extroversion, conscientiousness, relationships.

80. Who is someone that works and lives in a country different than his/her own?
    a. Immigrant
    b. Alien
    c. Expatriate
    d. Refugee

81. What is a stretch goal?
    a. A long term goal
    b. A challenging but not impossible goal to reach.
    c. A goal that stretches the entire organization.
    d. A goal that stretches the entire year.

82. What is task significance?
    a. The degree of freedom a person has over their job.
    b. The degree of variety in a job.
    c. The degree of which an employee performs a job from beginning to end.
    d. The degree which an employee perceives the importance of their job.

83. When an employee talks about unethical or illegal practices of their organization it is called?
    a. Treason
    b. Unethical violation of confidentiality
    c. Whistle-blowing
    d. Traitorism

84. An ethical school of thought where a person's right of consent, privacy, conscience, due process, and life must be considered.
    a. Justice
    b. Utilitarian
    c. Moral-rights
    d. Individualism

85. What is it called under the Equity Theory if a person feels they are being treated unfairly they decrease productivity?
    a. Change outputs
    b. Change inputs
    c. Distort perceptions
    d. Partial reinforcement

86. Which of the following is true of someone with an internal locus of control?
    a. They are typically more ethical
    b. They believe in fate
    c. They have limited accountability for their actions
    d. They believe things happen due to luck or chance

87. In the Two-Factor theory what would the pay and working conditions be qualified as?
    a. Hygiene factors
    b. Equity
    c. Relatedness
    d. Motivators

88. Which of the following reinforcement intervals results in very high performance?
    a. Fixed-interval
    b. Fixed-ratio
    c. Variable interval
    d. Variable ratio

89. The moral developmental stage where people learn to conform from the expectations of those around them is called the _____ stage of development.
    a. Preconventional
    b. Postconventional
    c. Conventional
    d. Esteem

90. Which of the following is NOT true about goals?
    a. They should be specific
    b. They should measure what means most to a company
    c. The time period should be flexible
    d. They should be challenging and realistic

91. Which of the needs of the Acquired Needs Theory would the need to foster closer relationships be:
    a. Power
    b. Affiliation
    c. Familial values
    d. Achievement

Use the below for questions 92-95
  I.   Transactional
  II.   Transformational
  III. Servant
  IV.   Charismatic

92. Type of leader that brings innovation by recognizing the needs of the employees and looks at new ways to solve existing problems.
  a. I
  b. II
  c. III
  d. IV

93. Type of leader that is characterized by their ability to motivate employees, inspire vision, lead by example, and are less predictable.
  a. I
  b. II
  c. III
  d. IV

94. Type of leader that is characterized by prioritizing the employees' needs over their own.
  a. I
  b. II
  c. III
  d. IV

95. Type of leader that emphasizes job-oriented needs over personal ones.
  a. I
  b. II
  c. III
  d. IV

Use the following for 96-99.
  I.   Recency error
  II.   Error of central tendency
  III.   Contrast error
  IV.   Similar to me error

96. The reluctance of a rater to give high or low marks.
  a. I
  b. II
  c. III
  d. IV

97. When an employee is improperly compared to someone previously rated.
  a. I
  b. II
  c. III
  d. IV

98. When an appraiser inflates the marks because of genuine like.
  a. I
  b. II
  c. III
  d. IV

99. When an evaluation is based on the employee's newest behaviors/accomplishments.
  a. I
  b. II
  c. III
  d. IV

100.   An employee who does not belong to the host or home country is a(n) _____.
  a. Third-country national
  b. Host-country immigrant
  c. Expatriate
  d. Repatriate

Answer Key

1. A. Doing a job because an employee likes it is an intrinsic reward (something that comes from inside).

2. A. The traditional school of thought is to motivate with economic rewards alone.

3. A. Outsourcing is when one country uses another country's labor resources.

4. B. The behavior method performance appraisal method is the most expensive to develop, keep relevant, and is susceptible to errors.

5. D. The 360 degree appraisal is the combination of various appraisals that give them employee and manager the best view at the employee's performance.

6. B. The peer appraisal is not an advisable appraisal method when peers are competing for positions or bonuses.

7. C. The manager/supervisor appraisal is the most traditional (but likely not most effective) appraisal method.

8. A. The subordinate appraisal is typically used for developmental purposes only.

9. C. A learning organization values teams and collaborative efforts.

10. C. Forced-choice is a rating method that requires the rater to choose from statements that best describe the employee's performance.

11. C. The halo effect is when someone is rated the same based on just a few attributes.

12. B. The job classification system is the job valuation system used by the federal government.

13. B. EAP would not cover the cost of cancer treatments.

14. C. HIPAA is the law that specifies after twelve months working at an employer with health insurance a worker can transfer to another employee without regard to pre-existing conditions.

15. B. Negative reinforcement is the removal of something unpleasant after a desired behavior.

16. B. Eustress is good stress that people feel when they want to accomplish something.

17. B. In a non-contributory plan only the employer funds the pensions (no deduction from the employee's salary).

18. A. Vesting is the period of time before the employer guarantees benefits.

19. D. The 401(k) is today's main source of retirement funds.

20. C. In the defined-benefit plan the amount an employee will receive is specific and not based on stock-market conditions.

21. D. Equity theory believes that people will strive for equality by changing inputs, outcomes, distort perception or leave their job.

22. D. Maslow's Hierarch of Needs theory focuses on several levels of motivation, the top (which few ever reach) being transcenders.

23. B. The hot-stove approach to discipline stress that like a hot-stove discipline be effective, consistent, and applied equally.

24. D. Learning organizations celebrate creativity and risk.

25. C. Mediation is the alternative resolution procedure that employs a neutral party to hear both sides and renders a compromise.

26. A. Open-door policy is dispute settlement with various levels of management.

27. B. Ombudsman is a designated employee that others can seek out to get counsel or resolution.

28. D. Resolution via successive higher levels of management is the step-review system.

29. B. HR must keep the I-9 for three years.

30. B. Adverse impact is unintentional discrimination.

31. C. Disparate treatment is intentional discrimination.

32. D. The four-fifths rule is the calculation in figuring discrimination hearings.

33. A. If McDonnell Douglas test is met, then a person can file a suit against an organization.

34. Career plateauing is when an individual stops advancing in an organization before reaching the highest rung of the organization.

35. C. Under OSHA law the third level is the inspection based on employee complaints of violations

36. D. The Fair Labor Standards Act identifies exempt and non-exempt employees.

37. B. The Landrum-Griffin Act gives state authority to rule on cases that the National Labor Relations Board will not rule on.

38. A. The Taft-Harley Act outlaws closed-shops based on union discrimination.

39. C. The Wagner Act grants the right for employees to form unions.

40. D. Religious affiliation has not bearing on whether someone is qualified for a position and cannot be included in a background check.

41. A. The ERG theory is a modification of Maslow's Hierarchy of Needs that focuses on three motivating factors.

42. C. The Two-Factor theory focuses on hygiene and motivator factors.

43. B. Theory X and Theory Y was created by Douglas McGregor.

44. D. The Acquired Needs theory focuses on achievement, affiliation, and power.

45. B. Utilitarian is an ethical decision based on the greatest good for the greatest amount of people.

46. A. BFOQ stands for Bona Fide Occupational Qualification.

47. C. The Davis-Bacon specifies a minimum wage for workers under federal contracts for construction.

48. D. A company with 50 or more employees is subject to FMLA.

49. D. Core job dimensions, critical psychological states, and the employee growth need are all of focus of the Characteristics model.

50. C. Task identity is the degree that a job is performed from beginning to ending.

51. B. The only question that can be asked for the ones given is if the applicant is a United States citizen.

52. C. Fair representation is the duty of the union to represent union and non-union members equally.

53. B. Repatriation is the process of an expatriate returning to their home country.

54. A. Paydays are associated with a fixed-interval reinforcement schedule.

55. C. Job rotation is when management moves employees to different jobs to give variety.

56. D. Job enrichment is the use of motivators (responsibility, recognition, growth) to increase job satisfaction.

57. A. Job simplification is the improvement of efficiency of a job that is typically met with resistance by the workers.

58. B. Job enlargement is the process of making a job more complex.

59. C. Unemployment insurance covers 26 weeks.

60. A. The WARN Act states that any business with over 100 employees that has a mass layoff plan must supply advanced notice.

61. D. Expert power is based on skills and specialized knowledge.

62. C. Coercive power is based on the authority to punish.

63. A. Legitimate power is based on the person's position in the organization.

64. B. Reward power is based on the authority to reward.

65. D. The three types of interviews are structured, unstructured, and stress.

66. D. The silver handshake is incentives for early retirement to avoid layoffs.

67. C. Constructive discharge is when the employer makes work-life so difficult that the employee has no choice but resignation.

68. C. The Age Discrimination and Employment Act covers people over 40.

69. C. A bonus would be an example of positive reinforcement.

70. D. Extinction is the withdrawal of a reward.

71. B. Negative reinforcement is the removal of unpleasant stimuli with the desired behavior.

72. A. Punishment is unpleasant stimuli for an undesired behavior.

73. A. The Hay profile method evaluates management positions based on knowledge, mental activity, and accountability.

74. B. Piecework is payment based on the number of units produced.

75. A. COBRA is the law that specifies that employers must make health coverage available at the same rate the employers would pay in the event of termination of employment, divorce, or death

76. D. Executive Order 11246 covers federal agencies and government contractors to comply with anti-discrimination laws.

77. D. Self-actualization is the utmost need on Maslow's Hierarchy of Needs.

78. D. Mental or physical limitation, documentation, and regarded as having the impairment are defined as a disability.

79. A. Extraversion, agreeableness, conscientiousness, emotional stability, openness to experience are the Big Five personality factors.

80. C. An expatriate is someone who lives and works in a country outside their own.

81. B. A stretch goal is a challenging but not impossible goal to reach.

82. D. Task significance is the degree than an employee perceives the importance of their job.

83. C. Whistle-blowing is when a member of the organization discusses illegal or unethical activity.

84. C. The moral rights is an ethical school of thought where a person's right of consent, privacy, conscience, due process, and life must be considered.

85. B. A person will change their inputs to decrease productivity as a method of coping with perceived inequity.

86. A. People with an internal locus of control are typically more ethical than those with an external locus.

87. A. Pay and working conditions are examples of hygiene factors.

88. D. Variable ratio results in very high performance.

89. C. The moral developmental stage where people learn to conform from the expectations of those around them is called the conventional stage of development.

90. C. Effective goals should have a set time period.

91. B. The need to foster closer relationships would fulfill the affiliation need in the Acquired Needs theory.

92. B. A transformational leader brings innovation by recognizing the needs of the employees and looks at new ways to solve existing problems.

93. D. A charismatic leader is characterized by their ability to motivate employees, inspire vision, lead by example, and are less predictable.

94. C. A servant leader is characterized by prioritizing the employees' needs over their own.

95. A. A transactional leader that emphasizes job-oriented needs over personal ones.

96. B. The error of central tendency is the reluctance of a rater to give high or low marks.

97. C. Contrast error is when an employee is improperly compared to someone previously rated.

98. D. Similar to me error is when an appraiser inflates the marks because of genuine like.

99. A. Recency error is when an evaluation is based on an employee's newest behaviors and accomplishments.

100.   A. A person working abroad that does not belong to either country is a third-country national.

9518065R0

Made in the USA
Lexington, KY
05 May 2011